For

# Music, Di<del>amonds</del> &
# Conspiracy
Fowkes and friends in India,
1701-1788

## Bob Fowke

YouCaxton Publications
Oxford & Shrewsbury

YouCaxton Publications
enquiries@youcaxton.co.uk

*If you have anything to contribute to the author's research or any comments
to make, please contact the above email and we'll forward your message.*

# Music, Diamonds & Conspiracy

In memory of Thomas Randal Fowke and Nancy Greg,
with much love.

# Acknowledgements

Thanks to my brothers Tom and Francis Fowke, to my daughters Emily and Fuschia and to my wife Pinney for their comments and encouragement, also to Toby Green and Philip Woolley, and to Shirely McLellan of Perfect-Proof who kindly edited the main text. Thanks also to the librarians in the Asia and African Studies Reading Room of the British Library whose kindness to the incompetent knows no bounds.

A special note of thanks to Ray Fowke from New Zealand whose *Fowke Family Tree* has been of great assistance. It is the product of a lifetime's remarkable and sustained research, consisting of three volumes in its printed form and now available online at Ancestry.com. I should also like to thank Professor Paul Edwards from Tasmania, whose paper, *Great Uncle Walsh*, gave useful insights for the chapter on John Walsh.

And a special mention for Eileen and Harry Green, both now sadly deceased. Their pamphlet *The Fowkes of Boughrood Castle* has been a mine of information and is beautifully written (small wonder, given that Harry was a script writer for *Z Cars,* the popular 60s TV programme). I have copied its second part as Appendix I without permission since I could not find anyone to ask for it. If you're out there, please get in touch.

## Main Characters

Randal Fowke, 1673-1745
Joseph Walsh, (?)-1731
Elizabeth Masquelyne, née Walsh, 1677- 1733
Joseph Fowke, 1716-1800
Francis Fowke, brother of Joseph, 1720-1802(?)
Robert Clive, 1725-1774
John Walsh, 1726-1795
Elizabeth Fowke, née Walsh, 1731-1760
Margaret Clive, née Masquelyne,1735-187
Francis Fowke, son of Joseph Fowke, 1753-1819
Margaret Benn-Walsh, daughter of Joseph Fowke, 1758-1836

# Contents

# Introduction

The archives of the East India Company and of pre-independence British India were transferred from the Foreign and Commonwealth Office to the British library in 1982. It was no small transfer—eight-and-a-half miles of shelves, comprising 70,000 volumes of official publications and 105,000 printed maps and many personal manuscripts. Among this huge mass of paper are two of the largest collections of personal correspondence surviving from the eighteenth century: the 'Fowke Papers' and the 'Ormathwaite Collection'. These two collections form an important part of the Library's collection of 'Private Papers' and are a rich resource for social historians, in particular historians of music. This book is based on those two collections but with reference to much other material also.

The Fowke Papers were bequeathed to the then India Office by Frank Rede Fowke[1] on his death in 1927. They comprise many volumes of letters between Joseph Fowke (1716-1800) and Joseph's children, Francis and Margaret, also letters of John Walsh, a close colleague of Robert Clive, and of others. They were rescued by Frank Rede Fowke from the family of the widow of his grandfather John Fowke, son of the Francis of the letters. John Fowke, a veteran of the Peninsular War, had ended his days living

---

[1] Frank Rede Fowke was the son of Captain Francis Fowke, a military engineer who designed the Albert Hall, much of the Victoria and Albert Museum and what is now the Museum of Scotland in Edinburgh.

on a barge near Newcastle-on-Tyne with his third wife, Jane Borthwick, the illiterate daughter of a local shipwright, and Jane had come into possession of John's papers on his death in 1851. They consisted of trunkfuls of mainly bound volumes of letters from his father Francis Fowke, his aunt Margaret, his grandfather Joseph and other family members dating back to the early eighteenth century. They were of no great interest to Jane Borthwick's descendants but they were of considerable interest to Frank Rede Fowke.

The Ormathwaite Collection was placed on permanent loan with the Foreign and Commonwealth Office by John Benn-Walsh, 6th Baron Ormathwaite, in 1958. (Lord Ormathwaite was the last of his line so the Library has acquired the collection in perpetuity.) The 6th Baron was the direct descendant of Margaret Benn-Walsh née Fowke, sister of Francis Fowke above, and the letters are between roughly the same group of people as in the Fowke collection. They are largely the correspondence of John Walsh, Margaret's uncle and benefactor, and the correspondence of Margaret herself, a highly intelligent woman, passionately devoted to her brother Francis and to music. As with the Fowke Papers, there is also a great deal of correspondence from earlier in the eighteenth century.

At the heart of both collections lies the correspondence of Francis and Margaret Fowke, devoted brother and sister, together with letters from and to their father, Joseph, and their uncle, John Walsh. All except Walsh were passionate amateur musicians and this common interest bound them together through many trying times - Joseph was a difficult man and a compulsive gambler although he was also very clever and boasted throughout his life of his friendship with Samuel Johnson. His brother-in-law, John Walsh, who protected Francis and Margaret after Joseph gambled his first fortune away, could also be irascible and difficult but he too was a man of 'great powers'. He became a member of the Royal Society in later life due to his work on the 'electric eel'.

It was unfortunate that Margaret, after her marriage to John Benn, her brother's secretary, suffered three still births before the birth of her first child, a daughter, in 1795 followed by her only son, the future 1st Baron Ormathwaite, born 1798. Perhaps because of this the 1st Baron grew up to be a spoiled and unpleasant man, hard on his tenants although very wealthy. He was once punished with a night-long session of 'rough music' by the villagers at Bracknell, their way of showing disapproval of his treatment of his wife, Lady Jane Grey (sic).[2] He was a prig and a snob and disapproved of his uncle Francis Fowke's choice of mistress, later wife, Mary Lowe, a woman whom he described as a 'common prostitute'. The rift between the descendants of the brother and sister is reflected in the separation of their correspondence into two collections. It is comforting to see the two collections now reunited under one roof at the British Library.

Margaret and Francis would have approved.

---

[2] Ford, David Nash,
http://www.berkshirehistory.com/castles/warfield_park.html

Map of the Coromandel Coast in the Eighteenth Century

# 1. Madras

The East India Company was granted its charter by Elizabeth I on 31st December 1599. This was part of Elizabeth's attempt to find trading opportunities beyond Europe after European trade had been limited by Elizabeth's excommunication by the Pope and by war with Catholic Spain.

In its early days in India the Company traded mainly from the Moghul port of Surat, north of what would become Bombay. On the south-east or Coromandel Coast, the Company traded initially from Masulipatnam, the ancient Indian port for Hyderabad where the Moghul governor or 'Nawab' (means 'deputy') had his residence. However, the English trading base or 'factory' in Masulipatnam was insecure, being unfortified and there were several attempts to find a better place to trade from. In 1626, having briefly attempted to trade from Dutch Pulicat, the Company built a fort at Armagon, just to the north of it. The new fort was badly constructed and its position was indefensible; it was abandoned six years later when they moved back to Masulipatnam. It was not until 1640 that Francis Day, the Company's agent on the Coromandel Coast, negotiated a charter for a fort at what he called 'Madras' with the Hindu ruler of Arcot - at that time, the Muslim Moghul Empire had not extended that far south. The name derived from a village close by and the fort itself was called 'Fort St. George'. It is said that Day chose this unlikely spot on an open beach so that he could visit his Tamil 'mistris' who lived in Portuguese San Thomé, five miles further south, so that their meetings might be 'more frequent and uninterrupted'.

Early Fort St. George was a basic square with four corner bastions, the outer walls each about a hundred yards long. It took fourteen years to build and cost £3,000 and the Directors in London complained about the cost every step of the way but it was a success from its first day. But by the end of the first year, up to four-hundred cloth workers had settled outside the walls and a motley collection of inn-keepers, merchants, servants, prostitutes, money-lenders and soldiers had moved up from San Thomé where Portuguese authority was in decline. Within forty years it had grown into a city of around sixty-thousand inhabitants, comprising Indian weavers and other trades and their families, Portuguese other European tradesmen and merchants, and less than a hundred Englishmen and English women. The English were always a minority in their own settlement. In 1678-9 there were seventy-four Company servants, of whom six were married and five had their wives with them - one English, one Dutch, two English half-castes, one Portuguese. In addition there were two widows and two unmarried ladies in the town – 'the women were as active in trade as the men'.[3]

The driver of this rapid expansion in population, far exceeding that of any other European settlement in India, was Madras's relative security and also English tolerance of differences of religion. Religious war was being waged on the continent of Europe, and a civil war with religious overtones had broken out in England soon after Madras was founded, but (in general) the servants of the EIC in India chose to turn a blind eye, sometimes despite instructions from the Directors in London. On reading letters that described battles between Royalists and Parliamentarians or, later, that described arguments between Dissenters and the restored crown, letters that arrived at least six months after the events they brought news of, it all seemed a long

---

[3] Spear, Percival (1963): The Nabobs: p13.

way away to the reader in India - and in all likelihood, things had moved on back in Europe in the meantime, so why bother.

On occasion, inevitably, home politics intruded. In September 1661 Richard Winter, a former governor, led a coup against George Foxcroft, the current governor who had been installed in office during the interregnum, because the Foxcrofts, father and son, showed republican tendencies. Nathaniel Foxcroft had said that he 'was obliged to maintain his private interest before the King's' and that 'he was bound 'to obey or serve the king no longer than he [the King] could protect him'.

But in general it was hard to take such matters seriously in the sub-tropical heat. In particular, it was hard to take religion as seriously as many back home would have wished. In 1675 the Directors, on learning that some English were being married, buried and their children brought up as Catholics complained of 'a thing so scandalous to the professors of the reformed religion that we cannot but disallow all such practices' and ordered that those who did not bring up their children as Protestants were to be sent home on the first ship, an order that was quietly ignored. In 1698 a new charter specified that every ship of five-hundred tons or more should carry a chaplain - and for the next sixty years only ships of 499 tons or less were sent out. By 1705 it was accepted that a rule against the appointment of Catholic officers was 'obsolete'.

Money was what mattered. It was noted by Indians, a little unfairly, that the English were unique among Europeans in that they 'never observed their own religion'.[4]

Madras in the seventeenth and eighteenth centuries was by all accounts a beautiful place. 'White town' dazzled in the bright sunlight. This was the area within the walls of Fort St. George where the Company servants and some others lived. The walls of

---

[4] Spear, Percival (1963): The Nabobs: p108.

its buildings were coated in 'chunam', a plaster made from seashells. It was so blindingly white that it gave people headaches and in the late 1600s an order in Council directed that the white should be toned down to allow some relief for the eyes.

For Europeans fresh out from England or elsewhere, the approach up the Coromandel Coast could be overwhelming. After six months or more at sea, they stood on deck as their ships slipped slowly up the golden shore, lined with wind-blown palm trees and framed below by the crashing surf, past the Danish fort at Tranquebar, past British Fort St. David, a subsidiary to Madras, past French Pondicherry sixty miles to the south of Madras and established 1680, until finally Fort St George came into view like a vision from paradise. William Dampier, 'Pirate and Hydrographer', described it in 1699:

> *I was much pleased with the Beautiful prospect this place makes off at Sea, for it stands in a plain Sandy spot of Ground close to the Shore, the Sea sometimes washing its walls which are of stone and high, what with Half Moons and Flankers and a great many Guns.*[5]

Madras was built on a spot that was completely unsuited to be a port. It lacked so much as a rigid pier to moor ships against until after 1815. Since there was no safe anchorage near the shore, ships had to anchor over a mile out to sea in the 'roads'. Everything - people, livestock and goods - had to be transported ashore through the crashing surf in 'masula' boats, flat-bottomed boats constructed from mango planks sewn together with strands of coir. The boats had no frames or ribs so as to have more 'give' and thus better withstand the shock of the surf, and they were rowed by a crew of eight to twelve men, including two for steering and two others for bailing. The experience of disembarking was nothing if not exotic.

---

[5] Love, Henry Davison (1913): *Vestiges of Old Madras:* Vol 1, p285.

Once on shore, newcomers would find themselves surrounded by crowds of Indian tradesmen offering transport to the Fort and other services of every description. The sights and smells were utterly different to anything cold grey England could provide, an England last seen at least six months earlier on the other side of the world, although the journey could take much longer.

This was the world that twenty-eight-year-old Randal Fowke entered when he first arrived on 11th July 1701.

# 2. Randal

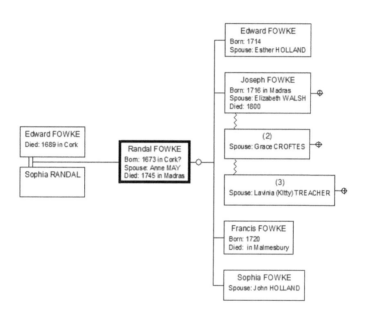

| | |
|---|---|
| | Edward FOWKE<br>Born: 1714<br>Spouse: Esther HOLLAND |
| | Joseph FOWKE<br>Born: 1716 in Madras<br>Spouse: Elizabeth WALSH<br>Died: 1800 |
| Edward FOWKE<br>Died: 1689 in Cork | (2)<br>Spouse: Grace CROFTES |
| Randal FOWKE<br>Born: 1673 in Cork?<br>Spouse: Anne MAY<br>Died: 1745 in Madras | (3)<br>Spouse: Lavinia (Kitty) TREACHER |
| Sophia RANDAL | Francis FOWKE<br>Born: 1720<br>Died: in Malmesbury |
| | Sophia FOWKE<br>Spouse: John HOLLAND |

Twenty-eight was comparatively old for a young man first setting foot on the sub-continent. Typically the young 'writers' for the EIC ('writer' from the Dutch 'scrivenor', an apprentice 'factor') were in their late teens or early twenties when they first arrived. However Randal's route to India was less than straightforward. He was born probably in or near Cork in southern Ireland in 1673 to a Dr Edward Fowke and Sophia Fowke née Randal, both from prominent Anglo-Irish families of the region.[6] Despite the 'Dr', there is no record of Edward having taken a medical degree so he may have been an apothecary, the jobbing predecessor of the modern GP. Unfortunately he was murdered in 1689, the year of the Battle of the Boyne when feelings between the Protestant settlers and the indigenous Catholics were running very high. Family tradition has it that he was dragged from his coach by catholic rioters on his way to visit a patient and killed on the spot.

Randal was twelve when his father died. He may have been sent to England and perhaps to London shortly after; the age for apprenticeship was typically fourteen and there were Fowkes prominent in the city, including John Fowke who was Lord Mayor during the Commonwealth; Randal's later employment by the EIC suggests London connections.[7] That having been said, his appointment was not straightforward and he was not initially taken on as a writer or trainee merchant at the Company's headquarters in London before he set sail, the normal procedure. Randal arrived in Madras in 1701 as a member of 'the gunroom crew' and not as a junior Company merchant, one of the elite of the community.[8] The Gunroom Crew was made up of sailors recruited from visiting ships and formed an internal security force; as near as the city got to a police force which was not very near at all. In 1732 there were

---

[6] There had been Fowkes in Ireland since the early seventeenth century when a Roger Fowke of Gunstone (1588-1649) in Staffordshire, who had twenty children, went out with the first wave of Protestant settlers under James I/VI. His fifth son, Edward (1629-1689(?)), was possibly Randal's father. Alternatively, Frank Rede Fowke (*Journal of the Royal Society of Antiquaries of Ireland:* Vol 2, p178) conjectures that his father was an Edward Fowke (1623-1689?) son of Thomas Fowke of Breewood also in Staffordshire (1582-1642), also mentioned in the Stafforshire Fowke genealogies. *See* Appendix II.

[7] Will of Randal Fowke: *see* Appendix III. There are small bequests to a 'very loving friend' Dr Charles Long, Minister of Chievely in Berkshire, to a Peter Bracknall, watchmaker of London and others.

[8] Love, Henry Davison (1913): *Vestiges of Old Madras:* Vol 1, p583.

sixty-eight of them: 'at the inner fort gunroom 8, at the salutation battery 21, at the new Powder House 12, at the Garden point 8, etc.'[9] It is safe to assume, given Randal's background and his later career, that his position as a member of the Gunroom Crew would have been that of an officer and one possibility is that he was initially an officer on a sailing ship, perhaps a second mate frustrated of promotion. There is no reference however, in any of the correspondence or in official documents, to him having acquired any nautical expertise before arriving at Madras.

There are glimpses of the colourful world that he had entered. In the year of his arrival, while he was still a 'griffin',[10] the Moghul general Nawab Da'ud Khan paid a ceremonial visit and Randal would have been on duty for the occasion:

> ... *about twelve this noon the nawab, the King's duan and Buxie were conducted into town by Messrs. Marshall and Meverell, the streets being lined with soldiers from St Thomas's Gate up to the Fort and the works manned with the Marrein [marine] company handsomely clothed with red coats and caps ... The governor attended with the mayor and dinner was in the consulting room consisting of 600 dishes small and great. After the dinner the company was entertained by dancing girls.*[11]

The following year, a Moghul army arrived at St Thomé within sight of the Fort with more hostile intent and Randal would have been involved in defensive preparations although an attack never happened. The year after that, 1703, he was discharged from the gunroom crew and taken on as a writer. It is reasonable to assume that this had been his ambition all along but circumstances led to his circuitous route to its achievement. This all took place during an odd time for the EIC in India. When Randal first arrived there

---

[9] Love, Henry Davison (1913): *Vestiges of Old Madras:* Vol 2, p.257.

[10] Slang word of the period for a new arrival during their first year.

[11] Spear, Percival (1963): *The Nabobs*: p20.

were in fact two companies. The monopoly of the original company had caused much resentment in London since its foundation; it was claimed that the East India trade was ruining England's manufacturing capacity and there had been a ban on Indian silk, a bitter blow especially to the Company's Persian trade. By the late 1600s, by which time the Company accounted for as much as a fifth of all Britain's overseas trade, there had been various attempts by competitor London merchants, or 'interlopers' as they were called, to break the monopoly. In 1689, the year of Edward Fowke's murder, the 'Convention' Parliament had legislated to allow interlopers some rights to trade to the east and a group of them met at Skinners' Co in Dowgate, subscribing £180,000 towards a new venture. This new company, known as the 'Dowgate Adventurers', evolved into something far more significant in 1698 when Parliament passed a bill setting up a new company based on the Dowgate Adventurers to trade in the east and foreseeing the disbandment of the old company. It looked as if the days of the EIC were over.

In 1701 when Randal arrived in Madras the old company was still in charge but was due to stop trading by 1703.[12] However in Madras itself the old company still clung to power under the vigorous leadership of ex-interloper Thomas Pitt (grandfather of the future Prime Minister) and the new company had been forced to set up its headquarters at the Indian port of Masulipatnam, whence the British had traded before moving to Madras and which was far from the centre of current activity. And things were even less straightforward than that: by far the largest group of subscribers to shares in the new company had been the Directors of the old Company, who had subscribed the massive figure of £315,000; and added to that, in addition to hanging onto power in

---

[12] Keay, John (1991): *The Honourable Company*: p180.

Madras, the old Company still owned all the real estate, the forts and factories scattered around India and the Far East.

Was Randal's desire to become a writer frustrated by supporters of the new company while he was still in London so that he initially had to take the lesser position of officer in the Gunroom Crew? He finally became a writer in 1703 under the aegis of Thomas Pitt, governor for the old Company, but it is unclear who was involved in suggesting him for promotion although the new company may have had something to do with it, for good or ill, in some way now lost to us. In far off Madras the distinction between them had become rather nebulous in any case.

The divergence into two companies was finally resolved in 1708 when new legislation ordered the creation of yet another company within which the assets of the new and old companies were merged to form a new united company. The EIC was effectively reborn and Thomas Pitt retained his position as Governor of Madras until 1709.

The Madras of the early 1700s in which Randal played the part of a rather old writer, still held only a small European population but it was blessed in being healthier than the other Company settlements in India, a place where: 'the inhabitants enjoy as perfect a health as they would do in England.'[13] By that time, of a total of perhaps eighty-thousand inhabitants there were only around seven-hundred Europeans and of these only 114 were English civilians: twenty-seven company servants, twenty-nine 'free traders',[14] thirty-nine sailors, eleven widows and eight maidens.[15]

---

[13] Keay, John (1991): *The Honourable Company*: p194, quoting the Rev. Charles Lockyer, 1700.

[14] Free traders traded on their own account in goods deemed outside the Company's monopoly. Free or private trade was also engaged in by the Company's servants; it was the main source of their fortunes.

[15] Spear, Percival (1963): *The Nabobs*: p11.

Together with the soldiers there were around four hundred English out of the thirty thousand and of these Randal was at last one of the Company servants, the elite of the elite and the raison d'etre for the entire settlement.

Given their small number and the fact that they were all male, the servants of the Company lived a collegiate life. All lived within the central fort, although a few senior merchants were married and also had separate 'garden' houses outside the walls. The gates were shut at night and all the Company servants ate communally at the Governor's table in order of seniority, Governor Pitt and the senior merchants at one end and the young writers at the other. The English, then as now, were notorious drinkers. And not just the English, the Emperor Akbar is said to have permitted the sale of wine to his English gunners because he said that 'European people must have been created as spirits and if deprived of them were like fish out of their element'.[16] The wine flowed freely and the unruly behaviour of the young writers gave frequent cause for concern. A letter from the Directors of 1710:

*We are sorry to hear of late that there has not been sufficient decorum kept up among our people, and particularly among the young writers and factors, and that there has been Files of Musqueteers sent for to keep the peace at dinner time.*

One wonders how Randal coped, being somewhat older and perhaps more sober than his fellow writers. He appears to have done a full stint as a writer because it was not until 1711, at the age of thirty-eight, that he became a factor. He would have lived in the 'College' or residence with the seven or eight 'hopeful young gentlemen' who were his fellow writers, all on £5 per year. The College was an old two-storey building which was locked at night

---

[16] Spear, Percival (1963): *The Nabobs*: p18.

to keep the young men in – so everyone used 'windows for doors and walls for ladders'.[17]

The Company hierarchy had been regularised in 1675 and at that time factors had received £2 per year, merchants £40 and senior merchants £50; the Governor and senior members of the Council £300. All this was supplemented by private trading, investing their own money rather than the Company's, which was the real source of wealth for Company employees. There were restrictions to reinforce the hierarchy, restrictions on who could use a palanquin, a sort of reclining sedan chair, and who could be followed by a 'roundel boy', carrying a ceremonial umbrella against the sun, and there was much pomp. The Governor 'never went abroad without eight armed peons as well as English guards, with two Union flags carried before him and "country music to frighten a stranger into belief the men were mad"'.[18] On Sundays he would process to St Mary's Church where the community awaited him, the short distance from the Governor's house to the Church being lined by up to two hundred soldiers. Within the church, the pews would be crowded with ladies and gentlemen and as he approached, the organ struck up and played on until he was seated.

Church was compulsory for the young writers and factors, and the Chaplain had high status with a salary of £100 and the use of a palanquin, and was accompanied by a roundel boy with an umbrella against the sun.

Once he became a factor in 1711, life for Randal progressed smoothly. He seems to have been well liked, a steady pair of hands. In 1713 he married Anne May, the ceremony conducted in St Mary's dappled light, built with a reinforced roof to withstand gunfire. We have no further information about Anne unfortunately and no letters from her survive. Children followed the marriage.

---

[17] Spear, Percival (1963): *The Nabobs*: p9.

[18] Spear, Percival (1963): *The Nabobs*: p6.

Edward was born in 1714, Joseph in 1716, Francis in 1720 and Sophia in 1723. These were the four who survived; there were five others who died young.

These were golden years for Madras and for the Company. Each year, between ten and fifteen ships set sail from London to return laden with Indian goods, sold for an annual profit of upwards of £1,300,000. The shareholders expected a dividend of 8%. In 1716, when Randal became a councillor and was one of the small handful of senior merchants, the outlook became even brighter. John Surman, the Company's delegate to the Moghul court in Delhi obtained a royal 'firman' or decree from Emperor Farukhsiyar in return for a large sum. This firman legitimised trading privileges in excess of what other European companies were allowed. The Company could now trade in Bengal, Bombay and Madras free of customs duties and could mint its own coins. News of the grant of the firman reached Madras early in 1717 and Randal would have witnessed the celebrations. A copy was carried through the streets in the state palanquin escorted by the Mayor and aldermen on horseback, with a company of English foot soldiers and 'all the English music'. At each of the city gates, the copy was held aloft and a proclamation was read. There was a celebratory dinner with a bonfire when the soldiers were feasted with tubs of punch and there was a 151-gun salute from the shore batteries – once Randal's responsibility as a member of the Gunroom Crew. The salute was taken up by the *Marlborough* and then by all the European ships in the roads, the ships hung with colours and streamers. The deafening roar of the guns continued for a long time during the afternoon, and the salute was repeated during a dinner at the Governor's residence that evening, where Randal's place was now near the top of the table, with additional cannonades during toasts to the Emperor, the King, the Company, and so on.

In 1724 Randal became Paymaster, a lucrative position. He wrote a report on 'economies' and was consulted about the Fort's defences due to his special expertise as an 'ex-artillery man'. In 1726 he reported on the western half of 'Black Town' beyond the Fort's walls, from Crosby Street to the Rampart. The inhabitants, he reported, were carpenters, peons, coolies and 'great numbers of beggars and brahminies who live in straw huts upon the sand on charity'. There followed a short spell as Rector at an additional salary of £50, shared with fellow councillor George Torriano, due to the sudden death of the incumbent, when he and Torriano would have conducted church services among other duties.

In 1728, aged fifty-nine he returned to England for a visit. From his first arrival in Madras in 1701 in the marginal role of officer to the Gunroom Crew, he had risen to be a senior councillor and a wealthy man. It was twenty-seven years since he last came home. He took with him his second son, Joseph, whom he left in England at school when he returned to Madras. He could not have been back in India much before 1731 at the earliest. Sadly Anne May died on Saturday 3rd August, 1734, while Joseph was still in England. Randal and Anne had been married for twenty-one years and her name precedes his on their common memorial stone outside St Mary's Church. She is described as having a character 'irreproachable, blameless and unspotted'. He was not alone for long however, if at all. In 1736 he had another daughter, 'Maria Flora', by a, presumably Portuguese, mistress of the same name, so he was not quite as unspotted as Anne was.[19] Indeed Joseph, his middle son, who wrote the words for the memorial some years later and there described his father, perhaps slightly defensively, as having 'the general character of an honest man', also suggested in his correspondence that his father was a gambler; but then, Joseph was not an entirely reliable witness.

---

[19] Will of Randal Fowke, *see* Appendix III.

Randal resigned from the Council in 1744 aged seventy-one.[20] By that time his three sons, Edward, Joseph and Francis, were all with him in Madras and doing well, as was his youngest, his daughter Sophia. Joseph had returned from school in 1736 and was a writer, Edward had married Esther Holland and became a councillor in 1736 and sat in court, becoming Mayor in 1738,[21] and Sophia had married Esther's younger brother, John Holland, a Company servant, in 1741.[22] In 1744, the youngest son, Francis, was described as a 'free merchant, living in Madras'.

The French had founded Pondicherry, fifty miles south of Madras, in 1660 and there had always been competition between the French and British settlements which sometimes boiled over into open conflict; for instance, in 1672 the French had stormed and taken St Thomé, five miles south of Fort St George, although they were forced to relinquish it. However, in 1745 the French had a new and ambitious governor, Joseph François Dupleix. Dupleix

---

20 Love, Henry Davison (1913): Vestiges of Old Madras, Vol 2: p313. *Petition of Mr Randal Fowke: I Having had the honour to Sit among You many Years, so many that I begin to think I can not perform my duty with that Satisfaction to my Superiours I have hitherto done. It is upon this consideration that I now humbly request you'll be so kind and generous to continue me the usual allowances to enable me to live up to the Character I have hitherto bore, without which my circumstances will not yield the comforts of life I have and shall be glad to enjoy without further Care and fatigue, from which if Your Honour, &c., will please to excuse by permitting me to Quit all Employs and Attendance, then will I sit down with my Hearty thanks to God, my Honble Masters, and all my Benefactors, ever remaining Theirs and your Truly faithful, Obliged, Obedient Servant, RANDAL. FOWKE.*

21 Keay, John (1991): The Honourable Company: p141. In 1672, a new Governor, Sir Josiah Child, had formed a municipal corporation in Madras on the Dutch model with mayor and aldermen and also adopted many Dutch terms: the apprentice factors were called 'writers' after the Dutch 'schruyvers'.

22 The connections between the Fowke and Holland families covered several generations, *see* Appendix IV.

was intent on expanding French influence and he was the first person to grasp that a small European force, used in alliance with native rulers, could transform the balance of power on the sub-continent. He had become governor general of all French establishments in India in 1742 and was backed by his clever Indian-Portuguese wife Johanna Begum, who had the 'eyes of a lemur' and was both attractive and efficient. Dupleix sought alliances with local rulers and wore extravagant oriental dress in order to impress them. He trained a body of native infantry or 'sepoys' to European discipline.

When the War of the Austrian Succession broke out in 1744, the British were rightly alarmed. The defences of Fort St George were in a dilapidated condition – the Company was always reluctant to spend money on repairs – but the situation was urgent and there was no time to apply to London for emergency funds. In 1745, Randal and his sons Edward and Joseph were among a number of prominent citizens who lent money to the Council, in their case 10,000 pagodas. The pagoda was a gold coin worth around seven shillings in the British currency of that date, the equivalent of a day's wages for a skilled tradesman, so it was perhaps equivalent to £100 in today's value (at the time of writing), in which case the modern value of the loan would have been around £1,000,000.

Randal died on 2nd October of that year while the crisis with the French was still building. His will (*see* Appendix 3) is typical of a merchant of the period and was signed on 4th July when he was still in a 'state of good health'. Edward, Joseph and Francis, were the executors and his estate was left equally to all his surviving four children including Sophia, now Mrs Holland. This equality of inheritance between the genders and the ages was common among families without landed estates, even those with substantial assets such as the Fowkes, where there was no desire to link land and name permanently by means of primogeniture. Of particular interest are a bequest to his beloved 'Cozen Martha Rogers in Cork in Ireland' and the bequest of a house to Maria Flora, daughter of Maria Flora deceased, and the sum of five hundred pagodas to be paid to her at the age of twenty-one, provided she 'embrace the Protestant religion', also five pagodas a month for her schooling and education until she got married. Maria Flora's inheritance was to be carefully supervised by his sons. Other bequests included twenty pagodas and her liberty to his 'slave wench' Minga, forty to her son Antonio and his liberty, and to all her children their liberty, also another 'slave wench' Magdalena got twenty pagodas. Domestic slavery was common in European households in India at that time.

Randal and Anne's memorial rests horizontally on the earth, forming part of a pavement along with other memorials in the dappled shade surrounding St Mary's Church where they married and would have spent many hours of their lives. The hum of the traffic of a great city now surrounds them. He had lived and worked through the 'Golden Period' of Madras when it grew to be the most important of all British trading posts in the East. Perhaps he did indeed have 'the general character of an honest man'.

# 3. Joseph Walsh and Elizabeth Maskelyne

*Joseph Walsh*

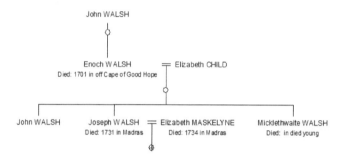

Joseph Walsh was born in Madras, probably around 1694. His father, Enoch Walsh, had become a writer for the Company in 1687 then worked as an 'accountant' in Madras, then as a free merchant. Enoch was the Company's 'supercargo' (representative) on voyages to Acheen in the Gulf of Tonkin (part of modern Vietnam) in the 1690s and made a fortune and he was already a good prospect when he married Elizabeth Child in Madras in 1690. They had three sons: John, Joseph and Micklethwaite.

In 1697 Enoch transferred to Bombay with his young family to be an accountant but Elizabeth died soon after and Enoch seems to have fallen to pieces. Bombay had come into the possession of Charles II as part of the marriage settlement of his Portuguese bride, Catherine of Braganza, in 1661 (the name derives from the Portuguese *'Bon Baia'*) and the British moved there soon after from the Company's original 'factory' in Surat, the Moghul port to the north. In Surat they had lacked fortifications, their factory being situated in the heart of the town where they were surrounded and vastly outnumbered by the native Gujarati population. Fortifications had become a necessity due to Moghul hostility, stoked by the piratical activities of English ships in the Arabian Sea.

Moghul disapproval continued after the establishment of Bombay, especially after the Company, under the feckless chairmanship of Sir Josiah Child, declared war on the Moghul Empire (1686), then at the height of its power under the Emperor Aurangzeb, an extraordinarily rash thing to do (*see* page 81); and all the more so after 1695, when an English pirate, Captain Henry Every (commonly known as 'John Avery'), captured two Moghul ships returning from Mecca. The first ship, the *Fateh Muhammed*, was owned by Abdul Ghafur, one of Surat's richest merchants, and the second, the *Ganj-i-sawaai* ('Exceeding Treasure'), was carrying Aurangzeb's daughter or granddaughter. The pirates indulged in an orgy of violence and many of the Moghul women were raped and some committed suicide and Aurangzeb was understandably furious. It was in this beleaguered atmosphere that the bereaved Enoch 'took to drink and dissipation and severely wounded one Ralph Hartley in a duel'. Although third in Council he was dismissed the service and in July 1701 he died on his way home, on board the *Tavistock* off the Cape of Good Hope, and was buried in a 'Great Tumbling Sea'.[23] Who knows, his ship might have passed Randal Fowke's going out. His three orphaned children became wards of a Mrs Anna Roberts of His Majesty's Yard, Portsmouth.

Enoch's eldest son, John, became a sea captain and then a diamond merchant. His middle son, Joseph, spent his childhood in England but returned to Madras, the place of his birth, around

---

[23] Eileen and Harry Green (1973): *The Fowkes of Boughrood Castle*: p4.

1716-18 as a writer. He had inherited a 'modest fortune' from his father and in 1721, aged around twenty-seven, he married a young woman called Elizabeth Maskelyne.

## Elizabeth Maskelyne

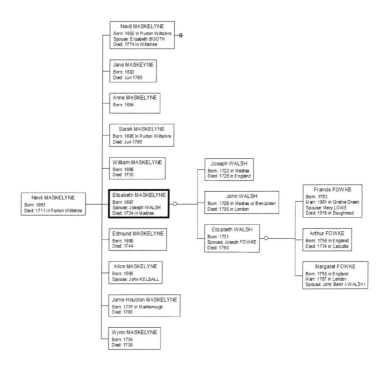

Elizabeth Maskelyne was born in Purton in Wiltshire (near Swindon) in 1697, the sixth child of Squire Nevil Maskelyne and his wife Anne, née Bath. By all accounts Elizabeth and her ten siblings had an idyllic childhood. All were dressed alike; many years later Elizabeth's niece, by then Lady Clive, described a tale handed down to her, that one day as the Squire's children progressed to church all of them dressed in yellow, an old lady seated on the church wall called out 'there go Squire Maskelyne's yellowhammers'.

Unfortunately, their mother Anne died in 1706 and Squire Nevil died in 1711. His eldest son, also Nevil, then aged nineteen, and the eldest daughter, Jane, aged eighteen, were left to bring up their younger siblings. Young Nevil was an excellent elder brother and ensured that all were properly educated and cared for, possibly too good a job because in 1720 he was obliged to sell Purton Manor and, in modern terms, 'downsize' to a smaller dwelling. Perhaps spurred by this, Elizabeth, then aged twenty-three, sailed to India that year in search of a husband, followed two years later by her younger sister, Alice.

There was nothing new about young women sailing to India in search of husbands; it was a practice far older than the Victorian 'Fishing Fleet' of popular imagination. As early as 1670 the EIC, concerned to fortify its male servants against the dangers of Portuguese arrack (a type of spirit made from coconuts) and 'foul women', decided to send out a shipful of young gentlewomen for the factors and officers and 'other women' for the troops, with one 'suit of raiment' allowed to each girl. Things broke down on their arrival: *'Be they what they will, at their arrival all pretend to be gentlewomen, high born, of great parentage and relations, and scorn to marry under a factor or commissioned officer though ready to starve.* [24]

The women who made their way to India were women of spirit. The young gentlewomen typically took over the 'roundhouse', the big cabin above the captain's cabin in the stern, and sometimes their 'dissensions might mar a voyage'. It was of vital importance that they practise their singing and their skills at the keyboard, usually the harpsichord at this date, skills deemed necessary to attract young men. The captain was absolute lord of the ship and had the power to enforce discipline, but with so many people

---

[24] Keay, John (1991): *The Honourable Company*: p135.

crammed in such a small space for so many months disputes and difficulties were almost inevitable. Robert Clive, sailing in 1764, complained of Mrs William Sumner who 'seemed possessed of every disagreeable quality which ever belonged to the female sex without being possessed of one virtue (chastity excepted) to throw into the opposite scale'. She played the same tune on the harpsichord four hours a day for months.[25] The journey typically took a little over six months but it could take a year or longer, as it did for Robert Clive on his first voyage which took a year and two months and involved four months stranded at anchor off the Brazilian city of Pernambuco due to an extended calm.

On arrival in Madras, most young women found the experience overwhelming: the sight of the gleaming white fort beyond the breakers, the Indians, the exotic smells drifting from land. Transported across the surf in coconut-fibre masula boats, the noise and confusion when they were deposited ashore were indescribable, quite a change from rural Wiltshire or anywhere else in England. News of the arrival of young women soon got around. Attendance at St Mary's Church the Sunday following the disembarkation of young single women tended to be more assiduous than usual, since that was the best opportunity for the men to get a sight of the new arrivals and possibly an introduction.

Elizabeth Maskelyne arrived in Madras in 1721 and married Joseph Walsh in St Mary's Church shortly after. We are fortunate that the earliest letters in the Fowke and Ormathwaite collections are those written by her. They are only a small fraction of all the letters she would have written during her life but we can hear her voice very distinctly. A hundred years later letter-writing had become almost an addiction among women of the upper and middle classes - they wrote thousands of them, sometimes several per day, and were often very good at it – but in Elizabeth's day the

---

[25] Harvey, Robert (19998): *Clive*: p300.

habit was less developed and her style is powerfully direct and a little naive.

From the evidence, Joseph Walsh and Elizabeth were very happy at first. The correspondence reflects this although death and distance lent an uneasy note from the beginning. In 1722 Elizabeth wrote to her older sister Jane, who had helped with brother Nevil to bring up their younger siblings and who would later, after Elizabeth died, bring up Elizabeth's children:

*Dear Sister,*

*I am safe arrived at Fort St George and believe you will be as much pleased to hear of my health as I am of this opportunity of returning my things to yourself and good Mrs Harwoods for the kind concerns and care you took of me at my departure from England. It was a great grief to me to undertake this long voyage without seeing you ... I have enjoyed a much better state of health here than in England and after some troubles and uneasiness which served only to make me set a true value on the happiness I also injoy in a worthy and tender husband. I leave you to guess at some part of my happiness when I tell you he is not ill in generosity, sweetness of temper and all the other vertues. I am sorry this time to write any thing that may give reason of greif and must tell you the unwellcome news of the death of poor Captn Tulley who died in two months after his arrival here of an inflamation of the liver and was followed by his cos Anne Kermyst in less than a month more who died of the same distemper. I pityed their fate but all must submit to the will of God. My best respects attend Mr Harwood and his lady who I hope are well and that you my beloved sis may enjoy good state of health and prosperity here and eternal ... hereafter is and shall allways be the constant prayer of your sincere and affectionate sister and humble servant Elize Walsh.[26]*

[26] Eur D456: Correspondence of the Fowke, Benn, Walsh and Maskelyne families: p12, Elizabeth Walsh to Jane Maskelyne at Mr Harwoods at Holten in Oxfordshire, 2nd Feb 1722, Madras.

Another letter to Jane shortly after describes the birth of Elizabeth's first son, called Joseph after his father. Unfortunately, letters took so long to reach home that there was a lapse of at least a year between the sending of a letter and the receipt of its reply and, not infrequently, people acted on information contained in a letter only to find later that the news in it had been superseded by events. In 1723, Elizabeth's younger sister Alice set sail, expecting to join her in Madras, but by the time Alice arrived, Elizabeth had departed for Sumatra, leaving Alice to make her own way (which she did successfully, marrying a Captain John Kelsall in 1724). The reason for Elizabeth's departure was that her husband Joseph Walsh had been appointed Deputy Governor of Fort Marlborough at Bencoolen on the south-east coast of Sumatra. Initially, Alice took the separation hard:

*… and now to be deprived of that pleasure for fourteen months longer which will be the soonest I can go is prodigious hard.*[27]

Things did not go well for Joseph and Elizabeth Walsh at Fort Marlborough. The local Bencoolen people resented the presence of Europeans among them and in 1725 there was an uprising and they burned the fort. The Walshes and the other British hung on in what was left of it and Joseph and Elizabeth's second son, John ('John junior' for now, to distinguish him from his uncle), was born there that same year but Joseph's star was sinking: he was dismissed from his post and forced to return to Madras while a Mr Macrae was sent out to 'unravel the tangled affairs of the Deputy Governor'.[28] Joseph described his distress to his elder brother,

[27] Eur D456: Correspondence of the Fowke, Benn, Walsh and Maskelyne familes p20: Alice Maskelyne to her sister Jane Masquelyne, Fort St George, (1723?).

[28] Love, Henry Davison (1913): *Vestiges of Old Madras*, Vol 2: p224.

John senior, by then a diamond merchant living in Hatton Gardens, London, in a letter sent from Madras, 14 August 1725:

> *Since [my last letter] have proved the inconstant state of Fortune's empire & by woeful experience tried the severity of her frowns ... from the highest point of prosperity & success I am reduced to the lowest ebb of poverty and want.*[29]

In 1728 Joseph set off for England to try to recoup his fortunes, taking their eldest boy with him in order to place him in the care of his brother John since Joseph now lacked the resources to pay for his son's education. John was to share the responsibility with Elizabeth's elder brother Nevil, although perhaps the real burden was carried by her sister, Jane, given that Jane had already raised or was raising her younger siblings. Elizabeth's letter to Jane of 10 August, which may have been carried by Joseph, is anxious:

> *.. but I am very far from it [good health] & the loss I am now going to meet with in parting with my dear husband which I fear will a long time retard my recovery and is a very grievous & hard tryall my Dr Sister, that I am put under to meet with so many afflictions one upon the back of another; to be robbed of our substance, deprived of my husband, any poor children exposed to an uncharitable world and myself left destitute in a place altogether disagreeable to me.*[30]

While in England, little Joseph contracted smallpox and died and his father Joseph was obliged to return to India alone in 1729, as a 'Free Merchant', no longer with the status of a Company servant although he managed to secure a position as secretary to

---

[29] Eur D456: Correspondence of the Fowke, Benn, Walsh and Maskelyne familes, Vol 1. p10.

[30] Eur D456: Correspondence of the Fowke, Benn, Walsh and Maskelyne familes, Vol 1, p 26: Elizabeth Walsh to her sister Jane Maskelyne, Fort St George, 10 August 1727.

Governor Pitt[31] on arrival in Madras. Joseph feared for his future. In a letter from Fort St George, dated 21 July 1729, he asked his brother John in Hatton Gardens to take care of his other son, John junior or 'Jacky', should things go further wrong. We have no clues as to the cause of his poor opinion of Nevil Maskelyne:

> *Your godson Jacky is striving to outdo his brother and if his strength of mind is equal to that of his body he bids fair for it ... Let me renew my request to you for the care of my child particularly that he be as little with Nevill as possible, for though I have still some esteem for that man, I know he is the improperest person in the world to converse with the child much, & the reason is very obvious.*

Then misfortune struck. In 1730 Joseph was found to have embezzled the Company of £7,000 in pagodas, a very large sum in those days. A letter from Elizabeth, also to John, asked for help for all of them and not just their children. She was already pining for home and no doubt Wiltshire:

> *... observing in a letter to your poor brother your kind request to him to put this lovely boy wholey under your care on account of the deficiency they say there was in the Company's cash, which, I must beg their pardons if I don't believe me of, or if there was any such thing that your poor brother had any hand in it there are many reasons to believe he had not ... and I believe he has not thought of writing about it till this year not considering that such neglect may be my ruin... I wish there could be some method found out for me to come to England with security to mine and my children's small fortunes for I abhor this place and long to be with my dear boy and other friends of whose comfort and assistance I stand greatly in need ... fearing my low and involved circumstances will*

---

31 Grandfather of Pitt the Elder.

*rob me of this and doom me for the remainder of my days to this detested place.*[32]

Things got worse. The following year Joseph Walsh died suddenly, leaving Elizabeth pregnant with a daughter, also called Elizabeth, and with serious financial problems. His memorial in the churchyard around St Mary's says nothing of what had transpired but Elizabeth's letter to John announcing Joseph's death, says much:

*I have come to curse the hour I was born, the fatall day when I set my foot on this shore in this accursed place and the more fatall day when the most charming the most honourable and the most excellent of all mankind conferred on me the highest honour and happyness, since that honour and happyness the transport of joy his matchless wisdom and vertue used to give me now only serve to press me down with greater wait of grief with agonising pain and despair to the grave.*

*Oh my beloved brother, I know you tenderly loved your amiable brother and that this dire mischance will pierce through and through your heart …*[33]

Governor Pitt made good the Company's loss from his own pocket but could not escape censure by the Directors:

The President is our cashier and if he trusts the key to anyone else he must be answerable … and although our President takes it upon himself to make good the deficiency, which was so far very well, yet the consequence of such an implicit faith in Mr Walsh might have been very fatal to him and to us if he had lived to

---

[32] Eur D456: Correspondence of the Fowke, Benn, Walsh and Maskelyne familes, Vol 1, p 42: Elizabeth Walsh to John Walsh, Fort St George, 30 August 1730.

[33] Eur D456: Correspondence of the Fowke, Benn, Walsh and Maskelyne familes, Vol 1, p38: Elizabeth Walsh to her brother-in-law John Walsh, 31 January, 1731/2 Fort St George.

continue the same evil practices … we will not permit the keys of our cash to be lodged in any other hands but the governor's.[34]

Five-year-old John Walsh junior was sent to England to be looked after by his uncle, leaving Elizabeth distraught and with a small baby daughter on her hands. She could not get over her grief, writing to her brother-in-law in a letter that accompanied her son, dated 31 January 1731/2:

> … *his lovely image is too deeply graven on my heart each minute of my life. I suffer the pangs of death more than 6 months have I been dying for him who can bear to be ages in dying oh gracious god look down with eyes of mercy. [The following postscript is in another hand, probably that of her sister, Alice Kelsall] My chief desire of this letter was to recommend her son to your care whom she has sent on this ship … she has not mentioned him nor is she able to write on any other subject so has desired I would do it for her.[35]*

John Walsh was taken aback by his brother's dishonesty, writing to a Captain Powney:

> … *your letters … which most sensibly touch me for the loss of my unhappy brother and I am much surprised no books or accounts can be found when I thought he was always most exact in those affairs … I am apt to think it's the effects of grief and melancholy has made her neglect it & keeps me entirely in the dark ... I have always had the greatest and most tender regard for the welfare of my brother in his lifetime so shall still continue all the good offices I am capable off to his widow & children & indeed I think she as deserving a woman as any on earth.[36]*

---

[34] Love, Henry Davison (1913): *Vestiges of Old Madras*, Vol 2, p252.

[35] Eur D456: Correspondence of the Fowke, Benn, Walsh and Maskelyne families, Vol 1, p31: January, 1731/2 Fort St George.

[36] Eur D456: Correspondence of the Fowke, Benn, Walsh and Maskelyne familes, Vol 1, p40: John Walsh to Captain Powney(?) on receipt of letter of 31 January 1731/2.

Elizabeth soldiered on in Madras. She had lost a husband and one son and the other son was now in England. All she had was her baby daughter and her health was deteriorating:

*Dear Brother,*

*… I have tried company, retirement and books, flew from one thing to another like a distracted person all to no purpose, still this fatall grief persues me and in every place like a cancer preys on my heart and drains my blood I am so changed you would not know me I look sixty years of age.*[37]

She died later that year and little Elizabeth, then aged two, was put on a ship for England to be brought up by her aunt, Jane Maskelyne, the same Jane who had helped raise her own younger siblings, those 'Yellowhammers' including Elizabeth's mother Elizabeth, all those years before. Elizabeth the elder left all her clothes and her slave girl Patty to her sister, Alice Kelsall (née Masqueline), and the remainder of her estate to her two surviving children. John and Elizabeth received approximately £2,000 each. All things are relative - despite the despairing tone of her letters she had been far from completely destitute. A letter from her sister, Alice Kelsall, to John Walsh describes the end and there were other deaths to report:

*Dear Brother,*

*… I must inform you of the death of my dear sister Walsh. She died on 24 November of a consumption. It is happy for hir she is taken out of her misery for she has been perfectly so ever since the death of her poor husband … I was not with my sister when she died which I am sorry of*

[37]Eur D456: Correspondence of the Fowke, Benn, Walsh and Maskelyne familes, Vol 1, p42: Mrs Elizabeth Walsh to John Walsh senior, Fort St George, 30 September 1733.

*for my poor sister's sake ... I believe I told you last year I had a little girl which I have been so unfortunate to lose. She died the 2nd September a cutting hir teeth. This is the third I have lost.*[38]

---

[38] Eur D456: Correspondence of the Fowke, Benn, Walsh and Maskelyne familes, Vol 1, p55: Alice Kelsall to John Walsh senior, Jan 1734.

# 4. Joseph Fowke and Elizabeth Walsh

*Joseph Fowke*

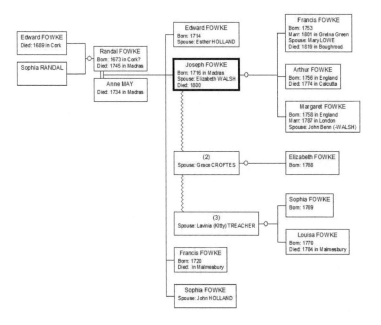

As we have seen, Randal Fowke and Anne May had four children, all born in Madras: Edward, Joseph, Francis and Sophia. Joseph, the second eldest, was born in 1716. There is no known portrait but we have a description of him as an adult, written by his future wife Elizabeth Walsh, whom we have just seen placed on a ship for England aged two. It was written shortly after their marriage:

*His person is tall and rather too slender; altogether has a genteel appearance; his eyes grey and small; not very bright but have a remarkable piercing look; his eyebrows are dark and very handsome; his nose is large but well made, his mouth is rather too large but not disagreeable, and his teeth are regular and of a tolerable good colour …*

There follows a description of his honest chaste temperament but also how he frequently fell into a passion:

*… but when he does so, it is to a degree of madness and even after it subsides his mind is in a most implacable state, out of which neither entreaties, condescensions nor endearments can draw him.*[39]

Elizabeth's description finishes with some lines about his high intelligence. There can be no doubt that Joseph was very clever but his life was far from straightforward.

In 1728, having spent his early years in Madras, Joseph, aged twelve, was taken to England by his father Randal to complete his education. He did not return to Madras until 1736, when he was taken on as a writer for the Company. His mother, Anne May had died, 3rd August 1734, while he was away and Randal had taken up with the Portuguese woman Maria Flora shortly after or perhaps before. It was two years after Joseph's return to Madras (in 1738) that Randal and his Portuguese mistress had little Maria Flora (*see* page 21).

Back in 1672, the Company had authorised the formation of a municipal corporation for Madras, complete with mayor and

---

[39]Eur D456: Correspondence of the Fowke, Benn, Walsh and Maskelyne familes, Vol 2, p 57: contained in a letter written by Elizabeth Walsh/Fowke to her aunts Jane and Sarah Masquelyne on the occasion of her marriage to Joseph Fowke, 1750, copied out by Joseph's brother Francis for the benefit of Joseph's son, Francis.

aldermen. The Corporation ran Madras in parallel with the Council and Governor, the Council and Governor having seniority over the Corporation. This form of 'local' government was on the Dutch model, imitation being the sincerest indication of competitive intent. In 1738 when Joseph returned, the Fowkes were well-established at the centre of affairs both on the Corporation and in the Council. His elder brother Edward was Mayor and his father was Second in Council and Edward also sat in the Mayor's court as a magistrate. The Fowkes were doing well but the political climate was becoming fraught. The largest native Hindu power to retain its independence from the Moghul Empire was the Maratha Confederacy which controlled much of central India. In the 1740s the Marathas were beginning to pose a threat in southern India and Nawab Safdar Ali, the Moghul Nawab of Arcot, sent his family to Madras for safety. On the 22 September 1741, John Holland, husband of Joseph's sister Sophia, was part of the party that greeted Safdar Ali with a salute of sixty-one guns.

*The 21st at Midnight the Nabob sent into Town his Mother, his Lady, and his Son, who is about four Years old. Their female attendance are very Numerous which has given us much Trouble to find room for them. The Nabob sent word that he intended to come the following afternoon - Mr Monson and Captain Hollond, the Polligar with two hundred peons and our Country Musick met him at the Edge of the Bounds. When he came to the Triplicane Bridge he sent back his force except about Thirty Horse … the governor attended by the Council met him the Fort Gate and conducted him to the consultation room.*[40]

The Moghul Empire, under Mohammad Shah Rangila, 'the Merry-Maker' (ruled 1719-48) was imploding and the War of the Austrian Succession had broken out in Europe the previous December, with Britain and France among the chief antagonists.

---

[40] Love, Henry Davison (1913): *Vestiges of Old Madras*, Vol 2, p280.

The Marathas were enough of a problem and Europeans in southern India tried to ignore the larger conflict although how long they could continue to do so was open to question: British Fort St. David was only five miles south of French Pondicherry and Madras was only fifty miles to the north.

That year Randal retired from the Council as we have seen (*see* page 18), pleading old age[41] and Edward replaced him shortly after. In his new role, Edward along with other members of the Council faced a threatening, indeed alarming, situation. A new and dynamic French governor, Joseph François Dupleix, had been appointed to Pondicherry and was in authority over all the French on the subcontinent. Dupleix was far more ambitious and more aggressive than previous French governors at Pondicherry, and Fort St George's fortifications were in a state of disrepair should he see advantage in extending the War of the Austrian Succession into India, thus fracturing the de facto truce on the subcontinent. In 1745, along with other contributors, Randal, Edward and Joseph Fowke lent ten thousand pagodas to the Madras government for the repair of those fortifications.[42] To put this in perspective, at this date a merchant's house would cost around one hundred pagodas for construction. This was almost Randal's last act for the city that had given him so much. He died that October, aged seventy-two.[43]

---

[41] Love, Henry Davison (1913): *Vestiges of Old Madras*, Vol 2, p313.

42 Muthiah, S. (2014): *Madras Rediscovered*, p354. The 'star' Pagoda (valued at 3.5 rupees and so called from the star on its obverse side) was the standard coin of southern India from the 1700s to the early 1900s. The Madras mint, established 1640, coined firstly Madras pagodas, fanams (36 to the pagoda), cash (80 to the fanam) and doodoos (10 to the cash). In 1742 the mint was moved and added Arcot rupees, star pagodas, gold mohurs, annas and pies.

[43] Some months after Randal's death the Council bought 'a house and godown [workshop] in Charles Street belonging to the estate of the late Randal Fowke'. Love, Henry Davison (1913): *Vestiges of Old Madras*, Vol 2.

Preparations for war accelerated: the Council ordered the construction of two swift despatch boats; a squadron of fighting ships was sailed secretly from Bombay; a granary on the 'Island', an area to the south-west of the Fort, was fitted out as a naval hospital. Then the French moved their troops to threaten Fort St. David and the British blockaded Pondicherry in retaliation.

Joseph Fowke was elected mayor of Madras in December 1745 during this state of phoney war, no shots having yet been fired, and things continued tense during the spring and early summer of the following year. Meanwhile Edward was involved in all the major decisions taken by the Council and their brother-in-law, Second Lieutenant John Holland, 'a gentleman of 40 years of age of great honour and good spirit and many other amiable qualities but never saw any other service than upon peaceable parades of Madras and St David',[44] was about to be put to the test. On 18 August 1746 Admiral la Bourdonnais, with eight French ships under his command, appeared before the town of Madras and fired a few shots into Fort St. George, also some broadsides into the *Princess Mary*, one of the Company's ships then in the roads. Following this initial cannonade, he cruised up and down in sight of the town and people of Madras. After two weeks of heightened tension, on 3 September Governor Morse and his Council learned that la Bourdonnais had landed his men somewhere down the coast and was marching on Madras. On 7 September 1746, the inhabitants of Madras woke to see a French army assembled on the landward side, where they were least expected. The siege of Madras had begun.

On that first day around a thousand shells fell on the town and the Fort although they killed only six people – but no one got any sleep and the 'lower sort of people' took the opportunity to enter houses that had been evacuated and got drunk on what drink they

---

[44] Love, Henry Davison (1913): *Vestiges of Old Madras*, Vol 2, p351-2.

could find. The European women and children took refuge in the Portuguese church which was built sufficiently strongly to withstand bombardment.

> *... on the first day of the bombardment all the black soldiers to the number of 400 or 500 leaped or let themselves down from the walls in the night and fled, so also the house servants and most of the slaves, insomuch the gentlemen and ladies could not get servants to kill or dress their victuals – going when possible to their houses to feed and get clean clothes ... 45*

Some sailors and others got over the wall into the Black Town, the part of town settled by Indians and various other nationalities such as Armenians, and fell to plundering the houses of those who lived there. There were so few officers in command of the Company's force which was made up of a number of English soldiers but mainly of topasses, men of mixed Portuguese-Indian descent, that John Holland and his colleagues were unable to control their men, inspiring some later and decidedly racial invective although not by John Holland.

> *The topasses of which the major part of the garrison consisted – black, degenerate, wretched race of the ancient portuguese as proud and bigoted as their ancestors, lazy idle and vicious withal and for the most part as weak and feeble in body as base in mind. Not one in ten posessed of any of the necessary requisites of a soldier.[46]*

By 10th September, Governor Morse and the majority of the Council had decided that continued resistance would be futile and they had better surrender on the best terms they could get rather than risk pointless loss of life, a decision that Morse's grandfather, no less a person than Oliver Cromwell, might have taken issue

---

[45] Love, Henry Davison (1913): *Vestiges of Old Madras,*Vol 2, p357.

[46] Love, Henry Davison (1913): *Vestiges of Old Madras*, Vol 2, p351-2.

with. In any case, the decision to surrender had a contrary effect: many of the soldiers and sailors 'hearing the town was to be delivered up, got drunk and all of them, drunk or sober, were for defending it'. In this stubborn opinion they had the support of only one member of the Council; Edward Fowke was the sole dissenting voice against the decision to capitulate. To be more precise, he was against the terms of capitulation. In a letter to the Directors afterwards, he explained that he would have preferred to lighten the ransom that was demanded by the French by means of a personal bribe to the French commander:

*In regard to ransoming the town, afterwards when Monsieur La Bourdonnais told us we might march out with our swords and hats, I thought it much more in your interest than to accept the terms that were agreed upon ... I have consented so far as five or six lacs ... Madras is but a tributary town, therefore for your honours to be loaded with such a monstrous sum, and the native government not to feel any part of so severe a blow, would, I am afraid, have a very bad effect, especially with a little money laid out among the great men, which the French pretty well know how to place ... I can assure you, gentlemen, notwithstanding I may have appeared so luke warm in defence of your town ... I would rather have sacrificed my life than to have acceded to those terms of agreement. I thought them as directly opposite to your interest, honour and credit as others thought them for it ...*[47]

When one of the ransomed bonds was brought to him to sign, he wrote on it:

*I acknowledge George Jones to have brought me the above-mentioned bond to sign, but as I do not approve the ransom, nor do I know whether*

[47] HEIC Court Records, Folio 5, Law Case No 31: Mr Edward Fowke, letter to the Directors, 25 December 1746.

*I am now legally authorised to take up money on the Company's account, I refuse to sign it.*[48]

To no avail. Morse sued for peace, guns were spiked and the guards withdrawn. French terms were surprisingly moderate, which was later quoted as evidence for la Bourdonnais having received a bribe: [49] the French were to take possession of the Fort and the Company's stores, and the British were to be 'on parole' and so would be able to move around freely. On payment of the ransom, the town would be handed back.

Later that day, the British watched as blue-coated French soldiers marched into the Fort, led by Admiral la Bourdonais. They disarmed the garrison rather brusquely but treated the civilians with tolerable civility. The French flag was raised above the Fort. Joseph's time as mayor is recorded as stopping on that day, when all Madras records stopped until repossession of the town by the British three years later, in 1749.

The British position had been abject, not because of any particular failing by Governor Morse who was probably correct in thinking that further resistance would have been futile, but because of neglect of the town's long-term security by the Company. There had been plenty of warning in letters back to London and in reports by councillors, of weak fortifications, lack of officers and lack of men. Under the terms of surrender, those in positions of authority who felt able to must swear an oath of loyalty to the French king and those who could not or would not must go to Pondicherry and were given four days to prepare - otherwise they

---

[48] HEIC, Court Records, Folio 5, Law Case No 31: Mr Edward Fowke, letter to the Directors, 25 December 1746.

[49] On his return to France, La Bourdonnais was at once thrown into the Bastille on a charge of collusion with the English in the matter of the ransom of Madras. After a trial extending over three years [1748-51] he was fully acquitted and set free. He died broken-hearted in 1755.

could give their parole (their word of honour or solemn promise) and might have passports to go where they pleased away from the fighting. A number of Catholics took the oath of loyalty with little compunction. In the meantime efforts were made to raise a ransom. Edward and Joseph Fowke lent 5,400 pagodas and Joseph lent a further 4,369 in his capacity as displaced mayor. French control was fairly unoppressive. Of the councillors, four, including Morse, were still in Pondicherry the following year, where they were quite well treated, and two were at Fort St. David. Edward Fowke moved from Pondicherry to the Danish port of Tranquebar once Morse sailed for England towards the end of 1747 (?).

Joseph himself made his way to Fort St. David. There he was joined by, or joined, Robert Clive, then still a junior writer, and John Holland who, apparently, had not given his parole and perhaps had escaped from Madras with Clive (*see* page 64) because he was soon involved in further fighting. Also at Fort St. David was John Walsh, whom we last saw aged five in 1731, put on a ship for England after the scandalous death of his father and shortly before the death of his mother. John had returned to Madras as a writer in 1742 where he had become friendly with Clive and Clive's future brother-in-law, Edmund Maskelyne, and the three young men had escaped from Madras together.

Accounts of life at Fort St. David during the following period can be surprisingly *insouciant*. During the French occupation of Madras and for several years thereafter, Fort St. David was the senior British fort on the Carnatic Coast, and the British despite their losses and despite the French being now in control of most of the Carnatic seemed to have lived there in a state of tense but convivial denial. There was music, dancing and gambling. John Walsh invited his sister Elizabeth to join him from England.

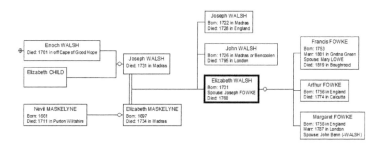

We last saw Elizabeth Walsh in 1734, aged two a year after the death of her mother, also Elizabeth. She was put on a ship for England two years after her brother John. Her mother had died in Madras the previous year, overtly of physical causes but perhaps also out of shame and sadness over the death of her husband, who had been found to have embezzled the Company out of a large sum of money. One assumes that, in the intervening period in Madras, Elizabeth had been looked after by her aunt, Alice Kelsall (née Maskelyne).

On her return to England Elizabeth had been brought up by her aunts Jane and Sarah Maskelyne at Pond Farm, in Purton Down in Wiltshire, and may well have been educated at Mrs Saintsbury's school in Cirencester which her cousin Margaret Maskelyne, later Lady Clive, attended a few years later. There are a handful of letters from a very young Elizabeth to her 'beloved aunts' in the British Library. They were effectively her parents.

> *Honoured Madam, My aunt Sara have got a crick in her neck so she desired me to let me know she received your letter …*

*Honoured Madame, I am very much ashamed that I have not write to you before to thank you for the sixpence you was so kind to send me but I don't love to write letters at school …*[50]

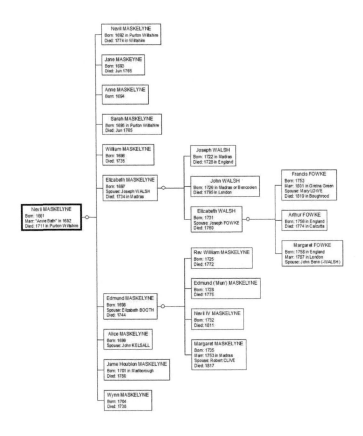

Jane and Sarah were remarkable women. Having taken on Elizabeth, they then took on Margaret, the orphaned daughter of

[50] Eur D456: Correspondence of the Fowke, Benn, Walsh and Maskelyne families, Vol 2, ps.67 & 68: Elizabeth Walsh, aged ten, to her maternal aunt Jane Maskelyne, London, March 30th 1741.

their brother Nevil and, later still, another niece, 'Jenny' Kelsall, orphaned daughter of Alice Kelsall who had followed her sister, the unfortunate mother of Elizabeth, to Madras and who probably briefly looked after three-year-old Elizabeth before she was sent back to England in 1734. Although of widely different ages and only first cousins, the three orphans – Elizabeth, Margaret and Jenny – were brought up almost as sisters, although Elizabeth and Jenny's time with the aunts did not overlap as much as that of Elizabeth and Margaret or Margaret and Jenny. And what a remarkable brood of foundling cousins the aunts managed to nurture: Margaret went on to marry Robert Clive and her descendants are now Earls of Powis; Jenny married Clive's secretary, Henry Strachey, and became Lady Strachey, ancestor of Lytton Strachey; Elizabeth Walsh, the eldest, married Joseph Fowke - and her fate was less fortunate.

Having received an invitation from Fort St. David from her brother John, Elizabeth set sail to join him probably some time in 1748. It was an exciting time for a young woman to embark on such a long journey. The War of the Austrian Succession was not yet over and there had been plenty of time for news of the fall of Madras to have reached England. Elizabeth knew what she was heading into.

We have no physical description of Elizabeth, only a note that her daughter Margaret was 'the very exact copy of her mother' and we know that Margaret was a tall, fair woman.[51] She arrived at Fort St. David on 7 February 1749 when it was still in quite a devastated state following an unsuccessful attack and bombardment by the French two years earlier, during which the British commander Stringer Lawrence had been captured and John Holland, the

[51] Eur D456: Correspondence of the Fowke, Benn, Walsh and Maskelyne familes, Vol 12 (cont), p136: Joseph Fowke to John Walsh, Calcutta, 3 October 1786.

Fowke brother-in-law, had briefly become military commander of the settlement.

> *We should have suffered considerably had not Captain Hollond, who has received a musket wound in the shoulder, with a great deal of briskness rallied our people who upon one smart fire drove the enemy away.*[52]

Pondicherry was uncomfortably close, Fort St. David being only ten miles to the south. So close that the British could hear the French guns when they greeted ships arriving. In a letter home to the aunts written shortly after her arrival, Elizabeth described her situation: the many houses that had been demolished for military purposes and how she and her brother were living 'in a house like an English barn … a little bedroom divided off at each end, and the space in the middle used as a parlour.'[53]

> *My Dearest Aunts,*
>
> *I was extremely seasick and kept to my bed for ten days. It was happy for me I was, for I never could have parted from my dear aunts without inexpressible grief … but I was too ill to think of anything & quite stupid. My brother behaved with the greatest tenderness; he kept by my bedside ... here are no houses hardly to be had you'd be surprised to see what strange holes people are forced to put up with. All the English houses were nocked down when the French attacked. We are obliged to stay in the black people's town … I have as many servants to wait on me as a duchess ... everybody has here. They are so intolerably lazy they can't stick a pin in themselves. It would make you smile to see your child carried along in a Pallanqueen like the Vauxhall boats by five blacks*

[52] Love, Henry Davison (1913): *Vestiges of Old Madras*, Vol 2, p387.

[53] Bence-Jones (1974): *Clive of India*: p26.

*and a soldier marching before with a sword in his hand and a boy
running by my side to keep my petticoats down.*[54]

Palanquins came with a close-knit team of up to eight bearers but
usually four to six, all wearing turbans of the same colour. The
bearers moved at a 'quick amble' and took turns if there were
enough of them. They were quite theatrical, often led by a
'soontah-burdah' carrying a silver baton about thirty inches long,
and some prestigious soontah-burdahs carried a 'chobdar', a silver
rod about four-and-a-half feet long. At night the team might be
augmented with 'link boys'. Elizabeth was perhaps attempting to
make sense of all this to her aunts when she wrote of a servant
marching before with a sword and of a boy looking after her
petticoats.

Servants seemed 'lazy' to eyes unused to Indian ways because
work was carefully divided between them; to do another servant's
work was to threaten his or her livelihood - wo betide a servant
who opened a door for his or her master or mistress if that was
someone else's job. If you were grand enough, there were servants
for every possible activity. There was a type of servant whose only
job it was to stand behind the master's chair at dinner. There were
many specialisms, for instance the 'hookah burdah' who looked
after the master's hookah and went with him to all social
gatherings, hookah smoking being an almost universal habit
among European men. The women servants or 'ayahs' were often
of mixed race. In addition there were domestic slaves, usually of
African origin and speaking some English, who were often given
their freedom (see Randal's will) but were sometimes badly
mistreated. To keep control of this mass of people and their
activities, every European household employed a 'banian' or

---

[54] Eur D456: Correspondence of the Fowke, Benn, Walsh and Maskelyne
familes, Vol 2, p70: Elizabeth Walsh to her maternal aunts Maskelyne, Fort St
David, October 10th 1749.

steward and a 'darogah' or 'gomastah', a general manager. Neither of these officials earned a salary and they made their income through commissions paid on transactions with local traders. They were essential because it was impossible for a European to grasp the complexities of Indian society even after years in the country.

Elizabeth loved it all. In another letter she described her gratitude to her aunts:

> ... *you who I look upon as part of myself ... my obligations are so great that to have but common gratitude no words could express it, but mine is the highest gratitude with all the love it is possible I can be capable of. Most high-flown style could not give you an idea of what I feel whenever I think of you. There are very few such in the world and I thank God for giving me three of them ...*[55]

## *Marriage*

When Elizabeth had arrived at Fort St. David, Joseph Fowke, then aged thirty-three, was already a counsellor and had previously been Mayor of Madras. He was a senior figure but not too old and therefore an attractive matrimonial prospect. He was perhaps a little out of his element away from Madras; his seniority had not protected him from attack by the Rev. Francis Fordyce, the extremely belligerent chaplain to the settlement. We know this from the testimony of Robert Clive. In January 1749, a week or so before Elizabeth's arrival, Fordyce had fallen out with Clive and made insulting remarks about him behind his back. Clive had confronted him in the street, where witnesses had seen the two men 'cudgelling each other'. Fordyce was subsequently dismissed

---

[55] Eur D456: Correspondence of the Fowke, Benn, Walsh and Maskelyne familes, Vol 2, p14, Elizabeth Walsh to her maternal aunts Maskelyne, Fort St David, November (?) 1749.

for insubordination having refused to accept the ruling of the Council on the fight. In his deposition Clive said:

> ... *that he is not the only person who has been abused and calumniated by Mr Fordyce who had also aspers'd the character of Joseph Fowke by saying that he was a dark designing villain, that he would slit his nose the first time he met him and that he had knocked him under the table at the governor's.*[56]

Joseph was a catch even if he lacked Clive's 'martial disposition' and had been 'knocked under the table'; he was both wealthy and clever and, at that time, he would have considered himself Clive's senior, Clive being still a relatively junior figure although rapidly making his mark. Joseph, while still a Company servant, found employment where he could at Fort St David and traded privately as did everyone. The Fort St. David having settled into a state of carefree merriment, as described earlier, a 'spirit of gaming' had taken hold, led by the governor himself. In 1750 Joseph Fowke was appointed one of several 'managers' with responsibility to bring the gaming under control, an unfortunate choice given his later history but indicative of his status.

Under the terms of the Treaty of Aix-la-Chapelle of 1749, Madras was returned to the British. Elizabeth and her brother, John Walsh, moved there later that year and found a house that was considerably more comfortable than the 'barn' they had inhabited at Fort St. David. Despite the additional comfort they found themselves living among the general devastation of Madras left by the French, in particular in Black Town outside the walls of Fort St George, where all Protestant religious buildings had been demolished. The destruction of Protestant places of worship caused understandable bitterness among the British. For years

---

[56] Love, Henry Davison (1913): *Vestiges of Old Madras*, Vol 2, p385, deposition of Mr Clive.

before the war, Catholics had found shelter in Madras and lived there with little prejudice against them, but during the occupation many of them had sided with the French. An order from the Directors in London instructed that all houses of collaborators be confiscated and that no foreigner of any nation whatever should be permitted to purchase any property in 'White Town', the area within the walls of the Fort, nor live in it.

Joseph Fowke moved back to Madras about the same time as John and Elizabeth Walsh. A council of five, subordinate to the Council at Fort St David, had been appointed to run affairs and manage the recovery of Madras and Joseph was 'Second in Council' under the Chief, Richard Prince. He successfully completed a courtship that he had presumably started in Fort St. David. He and Elizabeth were married in St Mary's Church sometime during 1750. In a letter to her 'dear aunts' dated 13th September Elizabeth told them the news and that 'Mr Fowke has an easy fortune ... and has been so kind to me to promise you a husband a year as long as we stay in India'.[57] That was not to be for long. Elizabeth was homesick despite the palanquins and excitement. In a letter dated 1 October 1750 she told the aunts:

*... and yet I am not completely happy nor ever can be whilst absent from you ... you tell me dear aunts that you see and talk with me in your sleep. I do with you almost every night.*[58]

She was perhaps still a little uncertain about her choice of husband. In another letter she described how their house had a view of the sea and how she was 'continually looking out for a Europe ship' in hopes of a letter from them.

---

[57] Eur D456: Correspondence of the Fowke, Benn, Walsh and Maskelyne familes, Vol 2, p19, Elizabeth Walsh to her maternal aunts Maskelyne.

[58] Eur D456: Correspondence of the Fowke, Benn, Walsh and Maskelyne familes, Vol 2, p27, Elizabeth Walsh to her maternal aunts Maskelyne.

Joseph also was ready for England. He believed he had accumulated enough money to secure them a genteel life if they were not too extravagant. (The loans to the Company for restoration of the defences of Madras and towards the ransom to la Bourdonnais were repaid in due course.) They booked their passage and set sail shortly after. Elizabeth was twenty-one and Joseph was thirty-five. By February 1751 the newly-weds had left St Helena and were buffeting their way towards Europe. Joseph sent a letter back to John Walsh in Madras, his new brother-in-law:

*Betsy is well but pinched with cold … I beg the favour of you to put my father's tomb to rights and I will send you an epitaph for him.*[59]

This was written as a postscript to a letter on 12 March at 2.00 in the morning, shortly before they disembarked at Portsmouth.

After the excitement of the last few years in India, the lure of 'home' was strong. They were followed there by Joseph's younger brother Francis, who had been a free merchant trading in diamonds while his elder brothers made their mark at Madras and Fort St. David. Francis's return was rather more adventurous and involved a hold-up by a surprisingly literate highwayman. The following accounts are taken from an issue of the *Gentleman's Magazine* of 1812, some years after the events they describe:

*Mr Urban Bath, March 17.*

*Ever pleased with contributing to your pages, I have enclosed you an account of three gentlemen being stopped and robbed by two highwaymen sixty-one years ago. The grand daughter of Captain Southby, who is now living here and has often heard her relation talk of it, put me in possession of it.*

*Yours &c. Fidelis*

---

[59] Eur D456: Correspondence of the Fowke, Benn, Walsh and Maskelyne familes, Vol 2, p30, Elizabeth Walsh to her maternal aunts Maskelyne.

The story which gave rise to the following letter from the highwayman Incognitus was this:

Three gentlemen returning from India, namely Capt. Southby, Capt. Forbes and Mr Francis Fowke, hired post chaises to get to London with all possible speed. Captain Southby was the only person who had anything of consequence to lose, and he had his whole fortune with him in Navy bills, which, if taken, might have kept him a long time out of his money, though it would have been of no service to the captor. To avoid such an inconvenience, he begged Capt. Forbes and Francis Fowke to assist in defending his property, which was cheerfully agreed to. They had only two pair of pistols between them. Capt. Southby, having the largest property, was allowed to take two. Mr Francis Fowke, who accompanied him in an open chaise, took another, and Capt, Forbes, in a close post chaise, possessed the fourth. Matters being thus arranged, they proceeded on their journey, meeting no impediment till they came to the bottom of Shooter's Hill about the dusk of the evening, when they were stopped by two highwaymen well mounted. An engagement ensued. Capt, Southby having discharged his two pistols, and Mr Francis Fowke his single pistol, the former called out for quarter, the highwaymen at this time having discharged two pistols. The leading highwayman answered, and bid him beware of using treachery, which he had given some reason to suspect, for that it was not usual for people to travel with an odd pistol. This circumstance being fairly explained, Captain Forbes, with a little reluctance, surrendered his pistol loaded. The highwaymen, finding no booty, could not be persuaded they would have risked their lives for nothing, and concluded it was concealed. With this idea they carried off all their baggage and left the owners tied to trees in a wood close to the road, where they would have passed a miserable night had they not been released by Mr Francis Fowke, whom the robbers bound so very loosely that he had not the least difficulty in disengaging himself, an indulgence which I think he owed to a very engaging and conciliating manner, which prepossesses everybody in his favour; and the compliment they pay him in their letter seems to favour my supposition. On taking leave of the prisoners, the robbers assured them if, on examination, they found everything to be as they had represented, they should not have cause to repent of their frankness. Mr Francis Fowke has observed to me that only one of the highwaymen was brave, and he, poor fellow! was afterwards hanged. Serjeant Lee told me that he supped with him after condemnation and on the night before his execution, when he behaved with a very modest and undaunted spirit. One cannot but lament that such a fellow was not employed in his country's service.

*Copy of a letter from Incognitus.*

"Sir – Pursuant to my promise to return the papers, you will find them in two different parcels, with the two seals and rings put into one of your wigs, and the picture, nigh the pathway from Marylebone to Paddington. Turn at the end of the first field, where you will see a close wooded bridge, and on the left hand, about thirty yards in the ditch, opposite to the eight line of dung in heaps, from which you will see, opposite, a little square terrace, which was a counting house to some brick kilns formerly – there you will find them. The delay has proceeded, I assure you, from a concern for your loss resulting from your courage and calmness, which are strong indications of a generous and good mind. There were several papers of different persons, which were of considerable value to them, for which you risked your life, as well as for your own; it seemed equitable that they should have paid a proportionable part with you, upon returning the whole things taken, which was intended without regard to the value of the effects, or the necessity of persons, and barely to the sum necessary to preserve reputation, which would have been very moderate, but I could not devise any manner to accomplish this, without many inconveniences, and without being known on an interview, or to such person as I should entrust, any of which circumstances I could not dispense with; for though, on information of character and humanity to others (for which I have grievously answered) you should pay me that great compliment of life, yet I must inform you it would be none to me, *for I would not accept of life with infamy. The sound of Highwayman is as detestable to me as to any man; though, without moralising on particulars, I cannot help thinking that you may see baser actions everyday committed with impunity in violation of every social virtue; and he that spares the necessitous in his power is not unlikely to relieve them; and he that will not prey on those who by toil and industry make even considerable acquisition, whilst he can from the superfluities of the opulent, though with greater danger, has a strong probability in his favour of being the more worthy person of the two; however, I must admit that example weighs much on the other hand. I shall only add, without any flattery, which cannot be presumed in this case, that your courage shall be no disadvantage to you, the effects of which I sensibly felt, though improper to be then intimated. It was my first expedition, and I have hopes to think it will be my last. Your effects, except some insignificant articles which are of no use to me, you may be assured, as soon as safety will admit, you shall receive without any gratuity. Our compliments to Capt. Fowke. I am, Sir.*

*Your most humble servant,*
*INCOGNITUS*
*Thursday, 19th September, 1751*[60]

At first all went well. Joseph and Elizabeth Fowke had around £18,000 and could afford to live comfortably. That year or the following year he was introduced to Samuel Johnson via Johnson's philanthropic friend and later lodger, the gaunt and silent apothecary, Robert Levet.[61,62] Quite how Joseph met Levet, who

---

[60] *Gentleman's Magazine* Vol 82, part 1 (Jan-June 1812) p334.

[61] Chambers, Robert (1998): *Law, Literature and Empire*, Wisconsin, The University of Wisconsin Press p.374 Robert Levet, 1705-82, from Yorkshire, learned his trade in Paris and became Johnson's lodger in 1762 when Johnson took him in after Levet had been duped into a 'bad marriage'.

62 Boswell, James (1831): *The Life of Samuel Johnson*, Vol 5, General Appendix, Letter 496, Samuel Johnson to Joseph Fowke Esq. April 19. 1783. *'You and I had hardly any common friends, and therefore I have few anecdotes*

practised in the seedier parts of London for modest fees, is unclear. Quite a close friendship developed between Johnson and Joseph over the following years, Johnson describing Joseph as a 'dear friend' and Joseph claiming to have visited Johnson every day of 1755. Joseph was good company by all accounts:

*His conversation was sprightly and entertaining, highly seasoned with anecdotes, many of which related to his great and venerable friend Dr Johnson. Mr Fowke once observed to Dr Johnson that, in his opinion, the doctor's strength lay in writing biography, in which line of composition he infinitely exceeded all his competitors. "Sir," said Johnson, "I believe that is true. The dogs don't know how to write trifles with dignity."[63]*

It was Joseph who witnessed Johnson's reaction to Lord Chesterfield's request that Johnson dedicate his *Dictionary* to him in return for £100, having failed to support the venture at the start. One morning Joseph called on Johnson and found him somewhat agitated.

*I have just dismissed Lord Chesterfield,' said Johnson, 'if you had come a few moments sooner, I could have shewn you my letter to him … however I believe I can recollect it pretty well.' And Johnson proceeded to recite a severe letter of reproof to Lord Chesterfield, chastising him for his want of support during the production of the Dictionary.[64]*

Joseph was still active in affairs. Much of his correspondence in the British Library is to John Walsh (hardly surprising, given that the collection had its origins with John Walsh) and their financial affairs were closely intertwined. It was difficult to return money

---

*to relate to you. Mr Levet, who brought us into acquaintance, died suddenly at my house last year, in his seventy-eighth year, or about that age.'*

63 *Johnsoniana, or supplement to Boswell, being anecdotes and sayings of Dr Johnson collected by Piozzi and others*, London, J. Murray 1836.

64 *Gentleman's Magazine* Volume 87, Part 2, p528.

from India and Joseph frequently requested John to spend money that Joseph had left on account in Madras, hoping to build up credit that Joseph could then spend or invest in England.

Joseph and Elizabeth lived in London in the early years. Their first child, another Francis - often known as 'young Fowke' to distinguish him from his father 'old Fowke' and to distinguish him from his uncle, also a Francis – was born on 25 October 1753 when Joseph was thirty-nine and Elizabeth twenty-four. Young Fowke was an 'uncommon lusty boy and looks as if he did not belong to either of us and begins to make a general fool of his mother'.[65]

Elizabeth was besotted. She wrote frequently to her aunts describing how 'Mr Pinky' had cut his teeth and other such momentous matters:

*Chickaree Biddy ... sputters and makes awkward endeavours at it [speaking] ... he is ruder and ruder every day and makes great fools of his papa and mama and of the whole house. I wish you could see him ... I have been to Reading Races.*[66]

Meanwhile, their money was running down and Joseph began to look for ways to return to India. By 1754 he was in negotiations with the Company to be made governor of Bengal and when things began to look hopeful, he tried to persuade Johnson to come with him. He had sufficient support in Parliament, always necessary since the interests of Company Directors and of the various political factions were closely intertwined, but he could not agree terms as he described in a later letter to John Walsh:

*You have no doubt heard ... that I was on the point of embarking for India. My proposal to the Company was a Nett Salary of £5,000 with*

---

[65] Eur D456: Correspondence of the Fowke, Benn, Walsh and Maskelyne familes, Vol. 2, p35: Joseph Fowke to John Walsh, 20 January 1754.

[66] Eur D456: Correspondence of the Fowke, Benn, Walsh and Maskelyne familes, Vol 2, p42.

*the common allowance of the table ... and to have all the land forces that should be sent abroad on ships of War or otherwise in the Company's pay, and under my command. The first the Proprietors would not accede to and the last the Ministry would not come in to. So, after many meetings ... my project was rejected, after it had lain with them four months.*[67]

At the time he put a brave face on it:

*My Dearest Jack,*
*... we neither of us repent our decision at our removal but we are obliged to study economy a good deal to make our Fortune hold out – I take more satisfaction in one day spent here than in a whole Years in India – I tell you I have had the Government of Bengal offered to me and I have refused it. Pray never let this secret escape you ...*[68]

The £5,000 per year 'net salary' had been his suggestion, he claimed, so that he would not be tempted to exploit the native population. It is not impossible that he was sincere in this; he was difficult man but not without honour. He was later offered the Governorship of Bencoolen, where Joseph Walsh had earlier come to grief, but nothing came of that either.

Life settled down. In 1753 the couple appear to have been living in Binfield in Berkshire, to the north of Bracknell, then they moved to Sunninghill, also in Berkshire.[69] They had another child, Arthur, in 1756 and a daughter, Margaret, in 1758. Their circle of acquaintances was limited and included Liz's cousin and childhood

---

[67] Eur D456: Correspondence of the Fowke, Benn, Walsh and Maskelyne familes, Vol. 4, p35: Joseph Fowke to John Walsh, 20 January 1754, London.

[68] Eur D456: Correspondence of the Fowke, Benn, Walsh and Maskelyne familes, Vol 4, p30: Joseph Fowke to John Walsh, London 22 December 1752.

[69]http://blogs.ucl.ac.uk/eicah/files/2013/02/Warfield-Park-Final-PDF-19.08.14.pdf

friend Margaret Maskelyne, now Mrs Clive. Robert Clive and Margaret had been married in Madras in 1753 and returned to London shortly after. The relationship between Clive and Joseph was no longer that between young writer and older, more experienced Company man as it had been at Fort St. David; Clive was now the more important figure following his heroic exploits against the French at Arcot and other places, all of which had taken place after Joseph left India.

Joseph's appetite for 'gaming' increased, along with his interest in music and his friendship with Johnson. His finances were in a bad way and most of his money was still tied up in India. Some trade with John Walsh went wrong. There were losses.

*My fortune is now reduced to £16,000 and I have £13,500 floating and ashore in India. Think what I suffer. Despair threw me into this situation … shadows will alarm a man circumstanced as I am.*[70]

Joseph was never one to understate his case. £16,000 was worth around £3,600,000 at today's (2020) value. Life followed, on the surface at least, a quite pleasant course. There were visits to Joseph's younger brother Francis, now settled in Malmesbury in Wiltshire, and Elizabeth lent 'Chickaree Biddy' to her aunts who were now at Cowley Street in London:

*Mr Frank [her brother-in-law] tells me you are lonely. If Frankie can be an amusement to you, send for him [from school presumably] but I think it will be better to return him at nights but do as you please …*

Little Francis was sent to a private school in Marylebone, 'I have a great loss in him, the Garden appears quite dull to me now. My dear fellow is not there to drive his hoop and climb the trees.' Then, in 1758, there was a respite. John Walsh, recently vastly

---

[70] Eur D456: Correspondence of the Fowke, Benn, Walsh and Maskelyne familes, Vol 4, p52.

enriched after Clive's triumph at the Battle of Plassey, gave or lent a substantial sum. Joseph thanked him profusely:

*Oh, my Dear Jack how cou'd you think of sending so much money thro such channels … The noble and generous Present you make me choaks all Utterance I am in the state of Cordelia, and can only say I love and honour you, and shou'd any Reverse of Fortune happen to you I will not be behindhand with you in Kindness … I am sure Clive will not want to keep you in India against your inclinations, and therefore I pray that no false point of Honour may deprive me of your company. My little family are all well.*
*Your Affectionate Friend Joseph Fowke.[71]*

But beneath the surface, things were turning sour. John Walsh returned from India in 1759 with a very large fortune, following Clive's extraordinary victory at Plassey, and by March 1760, the two men had fallen out bitterly:

*Sir, I return your papers and despise you and your Menaces. You talk and act like a man who has no idea of honour. I will tell you freely, I am upon Terms with you which allows the setting aside of all Connections and therefore as you have put out a threat, pray put it in Execution, if you have any Inclination for it.*
*I am sir, your humble servant, Joseph Fowke[72]*

The letters flew backwards and forwards between them. Their affairs were closely intertwined and it was hard to disentangle them. Elizabeth, caught in the middle, eventually took her husband's side. Joseph and Elizabeth returned Walsh's money.

---

[71] Eur D456: Correspondence of the Fowke, Benn, Walsh and Maskelyne familes, Vol 4, p 55: Joseph Fowke to John Walsh, Siddington, 9 December 1758.

[72] Eur D456: Correspondence of the Fowke, Benn, Walsh and Maskelyne familes, Vol 4, p47: Joseph Fowke to John Walsh, 21 March 1760, Cork Street, London.

Perhaps the strain took its toll. Elizabeth had fallen ill at the birth of Arthur with 'weak eyes' and a 'nasty lurking fever', now she declined rapidly. She died in 1760 within a year of her brother's return. Little Francis was seven, Arthur was five and Margaret was two.

# 5. John Walsh

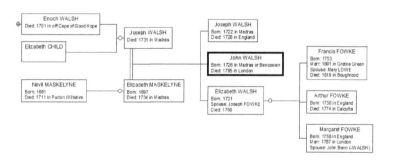

Wh

hen Elizabeth Fowke died, her brother John stepped in to help because sorrow had caused Joseph to lose control and he gambled his fortune away. That, at least, was the commonly held explanation, although we now know that his 'passion for play' preceded Elizabeth's death.

We first saw John Walsh when he was put on a ship for England aged five on the death of his father Joseph Walsh who had been found to have embezzled £7,000 worth of pagodas from the Company in Madras. Despite this and after the death of their mother three years later, orphaned John and Elizabeth each inherited £2,000. John was five years older but brother and sister were very close since they had no other immediate family. John was looked after by his father's brother, John, and Elizabeth, as we have seen, was brought up by her Maskelyne aunts, Jane and Sarah, but we can perhaps assume that John was a frequent visitor to the aunts in Wiltshire during school holidays, and the fact that his uncle cared for him does not imply that this was care in a daily sense. John may well have seen the aunts' house as another home. The absence of letters from him to them does not denote an absence of affection; in later life, he helped them financially.

In 1742, then aged sixteen, John returned to Madras as a writer, leaving his eleven-year-old sister in England. When Robert Clive arrived in Madras, also as a writer, three years later, John could claim some seniority over him even though Clive, at nineteen, was a year older, also John had inherited £2,000 which was £2,000 more than Clive had inherited.[73] This and John's sharp scientific mind meant that John, of all the close group of friends who followed in Clive's wake, was the only one whom Clive would listen to as an equal, especially in Clive's later years when he was ill and in pain and Margaret, his wife, had difficulty in making him see sense.

The group of young writers who were in Madras in the early 1740s had a very significant influence on Britain's rise to power in India from the part they played in Britain's rivalry with France. At the heart of this closely knit group were Robert Clive, John Walsh and Edmund ('Mun') Maskelyne, Clive's future brother-in-law who was also John Walsh's cousin, because Walsh's mother was Elizabeth née Maskelyne. Joseph Fowke, Walsh's future brother-

---

[73] Harvey, Robert (1998): *Clive*: p27.

in-law, who was in Madras at the same time, was ten years older than Walsh and was not part of this close group of friends.

The young writers lived together in a house set aside for them. They had to go to church twice a day which perhaps explains why they all developed into agnostics. They learned the local habits enthusiastically, which included chewing betel and smoking hookahs, and they visited brothels. The salary on arrival was a niggardly £5 per annum so they sought to make this up with private trading, trading with their own money separately from the Company. Life was interesting, although the work itself could be rather dull and involved much writing in ledgers with quill pens, and they were on the first step on the road to riches. They were part of the elite of the settlement and had access to the library in the Governor's house, a facility which Clive and Walsh in particular availed themselves of frequently.

When the French took Madras in September 1746, the young writers were obliged to watch powerless as the blue-clad French troops took over but they refused to give their parole (word of honour) not to escape. They were kept semi-prisoners in their communal house, as defiant as it was possible to be in the circumstances. In mid-October the French fleet departed. Walsh, still perhaps their unofficial leader, was the first to notice. He shouted from the roof: 'The French ships! They're leaving by God!' The others joined him and together they watched as the French ships set sail under a stormy sky, all cheering - to the extreme irritation of the French soldiers who ordered them down. The young men drank themselves into triumphant oblivion.

It was at this point that Dupleix, the governor of Pondicherry, took over command of Madras because Admiral la Bourdonnais had departed with his ships. Dupleix was far less accommodating than la Bourdonnais and conditions for the British became more difficult. The young writers decided to escape. One night, they put on the clothes of their Indian servants, blacked their faces and limbs and managed to talk their way out of the fort through the Choultry Gate, although for an uncomfortable moment a French-speaking topaz (a mixed-race Portuguese-Indian soldier) became suspicious and they might have been detained. Once clear of the town, they made their way fifty miles south to Fort St. David, walking far inland through the rice paddies and scrubland so as to avoid the main route along the coast and so as to give a wide berth to Pondicherry. It was soon after he had reached Fort St. David that Walsh, as we have seen, invited his sister to join him, and she was there by 1748, marrying Joseph Fowke in 1750, as we have also seen.

In 1749 when Madras was returned to the British under the terms of the Treaty of Aix-la-Chapelle, Walsh and another young writer, Stark, were ordered to return there. They arrived on 11th November and started work on organising its restoration. Madras had been badly knocked about by the French. Walsh was present at a first meeting of the 'Vestry' along with Joseph Fowke on 3 January 1750 and later that year he travelled back to Fort St. David carrying all the remaining official documents for safe keeping, those that remained after the French had left. The French had destroyed some and neglected the rest. For the following two years, while Madras was put back in order, Fort St. David remained the seat of British power in south India. It was not until 6 April 1752 that Governor Thomas Saunders moved from Fort St. David to Madras and Madras became once more the Presidency.

While Elizabeth and her new husband Joseph returned to England early in 1751, Walsh stayed on with Clive. He was in India later that year at the turning point in Clive's fortunes and in British power in India. The crucial event was Clive's heroic three-month defence of the Fort at Arcot against vastly more numerous enemy forces including French artillery, that and other equally bold actions. Clive, although not a blood-thirsty man and not a trained soldier, quickly established himself as something close to a military genius, and his friends, including Walsh, were not slow to acknowledge his fearless leadership and his unique abilities. Walsh became Clive's right-hand man for the next eight momentous years.

Another close friend of Clive was Edmund, 'Mun', Maskelyne, Walsh's cousin who had been part of the escape from Madras in 1747. Mun wrote to his sister Margaret who was being brought up by aunts Jane and Sarah in Wiltshire, the same aunts who had raised her cousin Elizabeth Walsh. In January 1751, Elizabeth, then still in Madras but about to be married to Joseph Fowke, wrote to the aunts to tell them that Mun had:

> ...laid out a husband for Pegg if she chooses to take so long a voyage for one, that I approve of extremely, butt then she must make haste, as he is in such a marrying mood ... [74]

Margaret arrived in Madras in a ship with eleven other young women in June 1752. She was seventeen. Following his military successes and perhaps arising from the strain he had experienced, Clive had fallen into one of his periodic fits of ill health and depression and Margaret nursed him for some of the time. They were married on 18th February 1753 in St. Mary's Church, Madras, and set sail for England ten days later with an assortment of wild beasts and Indian servants.

Meanwhile, Walsh stayed on and built his career. In fact, he never married although he had numerous mistresses. In 1751 he had been 'Rental General and Scavenger' and, in January 1753, shortly before Clive's departure, he became an alderman. By 1754 he was a senior merchant and 'under searcher at the Sea Gate', and in 1755 he was Mayor and was sent on a mission to Arcot with Stringer Lawrence, Madras's military commander. He was now in the thick of things and a senior member of the community. We

---

74 Bence-Jones, Mark (1974): *Clive of India*: p34 .

know something of his leisure interests at this time from a letter from Joseph Fowke. He had been sent claret worth £25 9s 6d and had a watch repaired for £21 16s 1 1/2d. A 'list of sundries sent to you this year' included: 'Shaw's bacon 2s.8-; Miller's *Gardiners Dictionary* 14s; *L'Esprit de Lois* 7s; *Sportsman's Dictionary* 7s; *James Dispensatory* 7s; Woollaston's *Religion of Nature* 5s; *Siècle de Louis* 14 7s; Shoemaker's silk 5,3d; Peruke maker's Bills 5.11.6; Pearl Barley 2s 6d; Bark 12s; Hatter's Bills 3.6 -; Charges of Ships 9s 7d.'[75]

Clive's return to England was frustrating. A seat in the Commons was then considered a necessity for any gentleman with ambition and he secured the Parliamentary seat of Mitchell in Cornwall, which was in the gift of the Lord Chancellor, the Earl of Hardwick who was the friend of an elderly Clive cousin. His timing was unfortunate however; due to the death of another member, if he had taken his seat the government would have lost its majority and consequently his election was overturned by the House of Commons sitting as a committee after a year of bitter debate, a not untypical example of eighteenth-century political practice. The day that his defeat was confirmed, disappointed and out of pocket, he accepted the post of Governor of Fort St. David and, on 5 April 1755, he embarked at Deal with his cousin George, and with Margaret and sixteen-year-old Jenny Kelsall, the third of the three cousins raised by the Maskelyne aunts, Jane and Sarah. Margaret was pregnant with their third child and she and Clive left two children behind in England to be raised by relatives. Clive and his young womenfolk made quite a stir when they reached Bombay. A letter from a Mrs Matheson to John Walsh describes them:

---

[75] Eur D456: Correspondence of the Fowke, Benn, Walsh and Maskelyne familes, Vol.4, p37: Joseph Fowke to John Walsh, 13 September 1754.

*Dear Jack,*

*We have taken Garriah the men at war stayed there some time to plunder and dig for riches Mrs Clive & Jenny's behaviour has not been very genteel here, you must know they set up for great wits and reformers and accordingly have ridiculed and lampooned everybody upon the place … Madame Jane rules their family entirely and both the colonel and Mrs Clive can not do anything without first asking Miss Jenny.* [76]

Jenny Kelsall was quickly married to Captain Thomas Lathom who was part of the fleet that carried Clive in an attack on the pirate fortress at Gheria, just south of Bombay. Once the pirates had been dealt with, Clive and his entourage, including the wonderfully flighty Philadelphia Austen, aunt of Jane Austen, set sail for the Coromandel Coast, arriving there on 22 June 1756, where they were warmly greeted by old friends, prominent among being John Walsh, Margaret's brother 'Mun' and Jenny Lathom née Kelsall's brother, Thomas Kelsall.

Meanwhile, a week before the Clives arrived at Fort St. David, twenty-three-year-old Siraj-ud-Daula became Nawab of Bengal, the Nawab being deputy of the Moghul Emperor and sovereign in all but name. Siraj was dissolute and cruel by nature but he was a clever and ambitious man who was determined to reassert Moghul authority over his upstart European subjects. He gave up drink and plotted his moves. Of all the Europeans in his domains, the British at Cossimbazar and Calcutta were the most problematic. A large proportion of Bengal's export trade passed through their hands and they systematically abused tax exemptions granted them by previous Moghul rulers, thus depriving Siraj of a substantial part of his revenue. Significantly, the British, partly in reaction to the

---

[76] Eur D456: Correspondence of the Fowke, Benn, Walsh and Maskelyne familes, Vol. 3, p11: Mrs Matheson to John Walsh, Bombay, 1756. Jenny Kelsall was Margaret Clive's cousin. When orphaned, she had had been raised by the same Masquelyne aunts who had raised Margaret.

capture of Madras by the French and partly because of fears about French intentions nearer at hand, started to renew Calcutta's fortifications - against Siraj's express order.[77] Siraj decided that he had to assert his authority. He assembled a large army, took Cossimbazar then marched on Calcutta, which he took on 20th June 1756.

British capitulation was abject. The Governor and councillors fled ahead of the people they should have been protecting and ended up on the tiger-infested island of Fulta, miles downstream at the mouth of the River Hooghly. Those left behind fared badly. Sixty-four British prisoners were crammed into the 'Black Hole', a small prison room set into the walls of Fort St William, where forty-three died of heat exhaustion after a hellish night, their sacrifice providing the British with a propaganda gift that was exploited for many years thereafter.

News of the fall of Calcutta soon reached Madras along with a plea for help from the Governor of Calcutta on his tiger-infested island - to which the Council of Madras reluctantly acceded. Stringer Lawrence, the Company's military chief, being judged too elderly and asthmatic, Colonel Aldercron, commander of a regiment of Royal Artillery then in Madras, was considered for the job but he refused to promise the Company a share in the loot. Clive, a Company man, was then appointed to lead the rescue mission. He was, 'the capablest person in India to lead an undertaking of this nature'.[78] He left Madras with a small British fleet commanded by Admiral Watson on 16 October, taking with him, among others, John Walsh, Mun Maskelyne, Captain Thomas Lathom and three companies of the Royal Artillery Regiment - which Colonel Aldercron reluctantly agreed to at the last moment.

---

[77] Dalrymple, William (2019): *The Anarchy*: p60-62.

[78] Harvey, Robert (1998): *Clive*: p165.

It took six weeks to reach Bengal, six weeks of atrocious weather when they were driven as far south as Sri Lanka, but by 2 January 1757 they were moored on the River Hooghly within sight of Calcutta having taken the Moghul fort at Baj-Baj twenty miles to the south. Calcutta fell to them without a fight but that was not the end of the conflict. Siraj-ud-Daula moved south from his capital at Murshidabad with a large army, all the while keeping up a peaceful correspondence with Clive, with the intention of lulling him into compromise. He was soon at the outskirts of Calcutta once more. In fact, both sides were playing for time. On 28 January 1757, Clive sent John Walsh and a Luke Scrafton to negotiate with the Nawab at the house of a powerful Sikh merchant named Ormichand where Siraj-ud-Daula was staying. The negotiation was tense and nothing was achieved. As evening came on, Walsh and Scrafton retired to their tents promising to resume the negotiation in the morning but they slipped away under cover of darkness. Either they feared that Siraj was about to turn on them or they expected Clive to attack during the night as he had done successfully at Arcot on more than one occasion, or they had discovered that Siraj was about to attack Calcutta, probably the latter. They reached Clive around ten o'clock that night and as soon as they reported to him he decided to attack there and then. The attack failed but 1,300 of Siraj's troops were killed and the rest of his army was demoralised and Siraj retreated northwards once more. After uneasy negotiations and manoeuvres over several months, there followed, on 23rd June, the Battle of Plassey which was the defining moment in the growth of British power in India. British victory owed as much to treachery in the Moghul camp as it did to Clive's risk-taking and military genius.

In all these events, Walsh was a key figure, at Clive's side throughout. Before Plassey he had been instrumental in obtaining the assistance of several hundred sailors from the Royal Navy squadron, then on the River Hooghly, to help move the English naval guns to a position whence they could bombard the Nawab's camp - his diplomatic skills were needed because Admiral Watson, as a servant of the crown and therefore not subject to Company authority, was almost as difficult as Colonel Aldercron had been when it came to cooperating with Company servants such as Clive. After Plassey, Walsh and another company servant, William Watts, were sent ahead to the Moghul capital, Murshidabad, 'to quiet the metropolis' and to make enquiries into the state of the treasury, a daunting task given that Murshidabad was larger and richer than London at that date, and stretched for five miles along the bank of the Hooghli and two-and-a-half miles inland, a dense bustling mass of narrow streets and low buildings interspersed with mosques, temples and palaces. Walsh was perhaps Clive's closest colleague, advising on the smallest details of policy. For instance, when Clive, who had followed with the army at a slower pace, was about to enter Murshidabad (29 June 1757), Walsh advised:

*It will be necessary for you to make some parade, music, drums and colours I think should not be omitted. Two pieces of cannon would add to the pomp and I am persuaded give no kind of umbrage.*[79]

There were very big handouts to the British leaders, Clive in particular but also John Walsh and others. Clive received £234,000, Walsh £56,250, and each member of the committee £27,000 and each councillor £12,000.[80] Walsh's £56,250 would be worth approximately £12,300,000 in today's (2020) money. It is interesting to contrast these sums with a letter from Joseph Fowke to Walsh written around this time but before news of Plassey had reached England. Joseph had come home too early and had missed his chance. The offer of the Governorship of Bengal was by then

---

79 Bence-Jones, Mark (1974): *Clive of India*: p144.

80 Edwards, P. J.: *Great Uncle Col. Walsh MP*: (P. Edward is Emeritus Professor, University of Canberra) for much of the following paragraphs.

a thing of the past, overtaken by events; it had become a very different and far more lucrative prospect than when offered to Joseph a few years earlier.

> *Dear Jack,*
>
> *I have received several very cordial and affectionate letters from you this year, but I am made too uneasy by the Situation of my affairs abroad to answer them in the manner I wou'd do; I must be short, and therefore can only say I am much obliged to you for your Friendship and am sorry it is not in my power to do you that service with the Company which your merit gives you a title to. I much approve your spirit & activity, as long as you have any left continue to be a doer. I am very sensible I have retreated too early in life; and my Head is in such a state now that I desire not think of undertaking any new charge. I have many things to say to you but writing makes me giddy. Pray … yourself in my affairs, for I really stand in need of your friendship. Shou'd my money come home to Advantage, I have still great schemes for you. If it fails, I am undone. God bless you and believe me unalterably, Your Affectionate Friend Joseph Fowke*[81]

Walsh returned to England in 1759 aged thirty-three, a very wealthy man. He reported on the state of affairs in Bengal to the Directors and verbally presented Clive's secret plans for reorganising the Bengal administration to Prime Minister William Pitt.[82] Both Clive and Walsh were aware of the absurdity of a commercial corporation such as the East India Company ruling over such a vast and populated territory such as Bengal; Clive suggested that he be authorised to accept the governorship and revenues of Bengal on behalf of the Crown rather than of the

---

[81] Eur D456: Correspondence of the Fowke, Benn, Walsh and Maskelyne familes, Vol. 4, p48: Joseph Fowke to John Walsh, 5 November, 1757.

[82] Edwards, P J: *Great Uncle Colonel Walsh MP:* Malcolm, John (1836): *Life of Robert, Lord Clive* op cit.

Company and wrote to Pitt that Walsh 'was a thorough master' of the plans. Walsh had evidently been involved in the drafting.

Once established back in England, Walsh lived mainly at his house on Chesterfield Street, Mayfair, his house being later the prestigious address of Beau Brummel, Somerset Maugham and Anthony Eden among others. In 1764, he also purchased and partly built Warfield Park in Berkshire in 1764, a stately home now subsumed into the suburbs of Bracknell. In February 1766, it was destroyed in a fire 'apart from the offices' and had to be rebuilt, a task that he undertook with enthusiasm, making additions to the park in the form of grottoes and terraces, lawns, ponds, lakes, a vineyard and a walled garden replete with peacocks.[83] Warfield Park was demolished in 1955 apart from the stables, and the whole area including much of the park itself is now a warren of mobile homes and other makeshift structures, a rather charming labyrinth of garden gnomes, carriage lamps and plastic flower pots. The ghost of Rachel, one of his many mistresses, is said to haunt the bridge over what remains of Rachel's Lake, named in her honour after she reputedly threw herself into its waters and drowned. She is reported to run screaming down Jig's Lane with Walsh in hot pursuit, an activity which, even if ghosts existed, would be highly improbable given his character - although he is said to have once shot a highwayman on Ascot Heath when riding back from London.

As we have seen, Walsh's sister Elizabeth Fowke died in 1760 within a year of his return and her husband Joseph went off the rails if he was not partially off the rails already. Joseph appears to have abandoned his three children – Francis aged seven, Arthur aged five and Margaret aged two – leaving them effectively orphaned. Although Walsh and Joseph had fallen out badly the previous year, Elizabeth's death brought about a reconciliation and

---

[83] Edwards, P J: *Great Uncle Colonel Walsh MP.*

Walsh stepped in to take over the care of his two nephews and his niece.[84] He had always been very fond of his sister (as were most people who had known her) and Margaret reported how 'after the lapse of many years, she remembered seeing him give way to a flood of tears in speaking of her.'[85] Walsh sent the boys to school in Cheam but they spent much of their holidays either at Chesterfield Street or at Warfield Park; little Margaret was brought up partly at Warfield and partly in the houses of her aunts Margaret Maskelyne/Clive and Jenny Kelsall/Lathom, later Lady Strachey.

Walsh was not an easy man; he was clever and autocratic. He became active in national affairs, if somewhat reluctantly. In 1761 he was elected MP for Worcester at Clive's request, thus becoming a central figure among the small group of MPs in Clive's 'interest' in Parliament, the others in the group being Clive himself (MP for Shrewsbury), Clive's father (MP for Montgomery), followed later by Clive's cousin George (MP for Bishop's Castle), John Carnac (MP for Leominster) and Edmund Maskelyne (MP for Penryn in Cornwall).

According to Clive there was 'no man in the world more attached to the Whig interest' than Walsh, although, Whig or no, he tended to put Clive's interests and his own inclinations ahead of party loyalties. For instance, in 1763 he joined with the opposition to vote against a bill to impeach the libertarian John Wilkes with whom he was very friendly. In 1766 he acquired a property at Pontefract at a cost of £16,000, which gave him control of another Parliamentary seat, and, in 1768, while he himself was

---

[84] Eur D456: Correspondence of the Fowke, Benn, Walsh and Maskelyne familes, Vol 2, ps 37, 47 &59.

[85] Edwards, P J: *Great Uncle Colonel Walsh MP:* John Benn-Walsh, '*Memoir of Margaret Elizabeth Benn-Walsh (née Fowke)*', by her son John Benn-Walsh, op sit (Mss Eur 032, India Office Select Materials, British Library, London).

returned unopposed for Worcester, he nominated Henry Strachey, Clive's new 'secretary', for Pontefract, thus enlarging the 'Clive interest'. Exaggerated accounts of their income were widespread and John was forced to publish a rebuttal. From after Clive's reappointment as Governor of Bengal in 1764, Walsh was effectively his representative in England and they were seen as close allies in the public eye. Shortly after Clive's return in 1767, when pressure on wealthy nabobs was growing in Parliament and in the country, Clive appeared in a lampoon as 'Lord Vulture' with Walsh beside him as 'Skeleton Scarecrow'.

However, over time he grew to disapprove of Clive's more self-interested political manoeuvres and became increasingly uneasy about the political aspects of their relationship. They had originally supported the ministry of William Pitt and the Duke of Newcastle but when Clive changed ship, Walsh felt unable to follow him and wrote from Chesterfield Street:

*Dear Lord Clive,*

*... I have long been & shall remain inviolably attached to you, as well from affection as from Gratitude. I entered into Parliament, chiefly with the view of being serviceable to you, & as you know have ever since acted entirely with you, that is, in support of the Duke of Newcastle and Mr Pitt ... if it is required of you to bring me over with you, all I can do is to resign my seat in Parliament, which I readily will, if it is essential to your Interests. I wish you success in your Election & hope your friends use the utmost caution with respect to Bribery, every detection of which will subject them to £500 penalty, & endanger the election upon petition. My love to Lady Clive & compliments to George, Harry etc . I am my dear Lord, your very affectionate humble servant, John Walsh.*[86]

---

86 Edwards, P J: *Great Uncle Colonel Walsh MP*: Malcolm, John (1836): *Life of Robert, Lord Clive*, John Murray op cit.

In fact, he did not resign his seat but continued to divide his time between Parliament, which he was not very assiduous in attending, and visits to friends and relatives and to resorts such as Bath or Brighton. In addition to this, there were his mistresses and his scientific interests.

Clive's health became increasingly precarious as did his mental state. He was given to bouts of depression and, in modern parlance, we might diagnose post-traumatic stress disorder, given that he had risked his life on many occasions. Walsh was an essential support. Out of respect for Walsh's scientific turn of mind, Clive would listen to Walsh's advice while discounting that of most other people. A typically witty letter from Margaret written '10.00 at night, Thursday' [September 1770] gives a flavour of this close relationship:

> … *All's well, & yet you are not here! How could you refuse coming? Out of revenge Lord Clive is grown wonderfully well & we are in good spirits ..*
> *Your affectionate cousin M. Clive*
> *'Do not expect us. We chose to stay at Walcot. Goodby t'ye.*[87]

In October 1764, Nevil Maskelyne, Margaret's younger brother, had stayed with Walsh in Chesterfield Street on Nevil's return from an expedition to Barbados to test marine chronometers (part of the search for a means of calculating longitude). When the incumbent Astronomer Royal died the following year, Nevil succeeded to the position with help from Walsh, who used his influence to win the support of Grenville, the then Prime Minister and Lord Sandwich, the Secretary of State. In return, in 1770,

---

[87] Eur D456: Correspondence of the Fowke, Benn, Walsh and Maskelyne families, Vol. 8-9, p10: Lady Clive to John Walsh, Walcot, '10 at night Thursday 1770'.

Nevil, who was already a Fellow of the Royal Society, and Dr Benjamin Franklin, who would become Walsh's scientific mentor, proposed him to the Society and Walsh was elected with the support of seven other Fellows, of whom four were also fellows of the Society of Antiquarians to which he was also elected. Nevil Maskelyne described him as 'a Gentleman well acquainted with philosophical & polite literature, & particularly versed in the natural history and antiquities of India'.[88] His nephew, Arthur Fowke, noted how his uncle's scientific interests had begun to take precedence over other matters: 'on a Thursday evening my Uncle generally carries Mr Davies to the Royal Society ...'[89]

Of the two Fowke boys, Arthur, who was as clever as his elder brother, Francis, became most involved in his uncle's scientific interests, writing to his sister Margaret from Chesterfield Street:

> *I have read through Priestly's book and am now engaged on Franklin's letters concerning electricity ... by the little I have seen of him he seems to be a very sociable and agreeable companion. He dined here a few days ago. I have lately begun to learn to ride and to fence.*[90]

Fifteen-year-old Arthur, together with his tutor David Davies, accompanied Walsh to Brittany in the summer of 1772 where they carried out a series of historic experiments on electric fish. Walsh summarised the initial results of these experiments in a letter to Benjamin Franklin from the town of La Rochelle. His letter was read to the Royal Society by president Sir John Pringle a year later and published in the society's journal and it earned Walsh the

---

[88] Edwards, P J: *Great Uncle Colonel Walsh MP:* op sit Royal Society archives: www2.royalsociety.org/DServe

[89] EUR, Minor Collections, Fowke Mss, p80: Arthur Fowke to sister Margaret, Chesterfield Street, Feb 13, 1772.

[90] EUR, Minor Collections, Fowke Mss, p 80: Arthur Fowke to sister Margaret, Chesterfield Street, Feb 13, 1772.

Society's prestigious Copley Medal.[91] He and his two assistants had succeeded in proving beyond doubt the electrical origin of the numbing sensation induced by the Torpedo Ray, a mysterious phenomenon known to the ancient Greeks and Romans. As Walsh wrote to Benjamin Franklin "…the effect of the Torpedo appears to be absolutely electrical".

The expedition to Brittany was not without incident. Walsh was known to the French authorities as an MP and probably also as an officer in the Worcester militia and as a former military assistant to Clive, the man largely responsible for the collapse of French influence in India. It is not altogether surprising that two days after writing to Franklin and moving his party to nearby the Ile de Ré, a fortified island, Walsh was threatened with arrest and forbidden to take further measurements. He was ordered to leave the island but then the order was withdrawn without explanation and, at the end of their stay, he received an unexpected invitation to dine with the military governor as guest of honour.

On withdrawal of the order, the earlier incident was treated as an unfortunate misunderstanding and Walsh demonstrated the electrical nature of the torpedo's shocks to the governor and forty of his officers together with local civic dignitaries.[92] His demonstration - that transmission of the Torpedo's shocks required a closed electric circuit - attracted enormous public interest in Paris and London. We now know that the torpedo ray acts like a fifty-volt electric battery, driving a current of about one amp through sea water, sufficient to stun and immobilise nearby predators and prey. We get a glimpse of Walsh around this time in

---

[91] Walsh, John (1773): *Of The Electric Property of the Torpedo*: The Philosophical Transactions, Royal Society of London.

[92] Edwards, P J: *Great Uncle Colonel Walsh MP:* Piccolino, Marco (2003): *The Taming of the Ray*: p84 Leo S. Olschki, Florence, 2003, op sit.

a letter from Edward Fowke to Arthur Fowke's elder brother Francis:

*I have been in company with Mr Walsh but once since you left me, and Peggy you know I hardly ever see. About 1 o'Clock today he saluted me at my Window from his horse with one his Pleasantest smiles, which would make him more agreeable could he oftener wear. The old boy keeps to his fashionable Wigg …* [93]

Margaret Clive, whose own interests were music and astronomy, continued to rely on Walsh whenever Clive was ill or depressed and Clive himself continued to make use of him. In 1772, along with Clive's new secretary, Henry Strachey, recently married to Jenny Kelsall/Lathom (Captain Lathom had died), Walsh gave evidence to the select committee set up by Parliament to investigate Clive's affairs of an attempt by Clive's enemies to prosecute him. Following this, Walsh was closely involved in Clive's trial in Parliament in 1773, the prosecution led by Edmund Burke's associate 'Gentleman Johnny' Burgoyne. [94]

Clive died at his house in Berkley Square on 22nd November 1774, probably suicide. In October, he had caught a cold when fishing in the River Teme at Oakley Park in Shropshire, the infection took hold and he had difficulty swallowing. After a hideously uncomfortable journey he arrived at his house in Berkley Square and told Margaret that he was dying. He had acute stomach

[93] Eur D456: Correspondence of the Fowke, Benn, Walsh and Maskelyne families, Vol. 31, p 71: Edward Fowke to his nephew Francis Fowke, Curzon Street, 26 January 1773.

[94] George Bernard Shaw made General Burgoyne the subject of his play *Arms and the Man*, which is based around events during the American War of Independence where Burgoyne lost the decisive Battle of Saratoga. Interestingly, Clive might have been called upon to lead British forces in the north rather than Burgoyne, in which case the outcome might have been very different – except that Clive was more sympathetic towards the Americans so this was never really on the cards.

pains and was impossible, moaning and shouting and depressed. He probably cut his throat with a small penknife one evening when Margaret and a few family and friends were in the drawing room. Probably to avoid news of the scandal of suicide seeping out and because suicides were refused burial in sacred ground, his body was carried secretly to Morton Saye in Shropshire, his birthplace, in a cavalcade of coaches carrying Margaret, Jenny Strachey and others, thundering through the night. He was buried anonymously under the nave of the church.

Following Clive's death, Walsh continued on friendly terms with Margaret although he fell out with Clive's rather slow-witted son, Edmund, who refused to reimburse him for his expenses when standing as an MP for Worcester in Clive's interest, which may or may not have been an unreasonable request by Walsh but was a small price to pay to retain the friendship of a such a close acquaintance of Edmund's famous father.

# 6. Calcutta

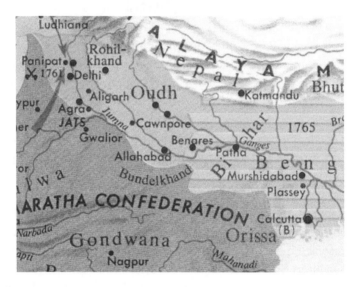

Calcutta was founded in 1690, fifty years after the founding of Madras, but whereas the founding of Madras was peacefully negotiated with the Rajah of Arcot (1640), the founding of Calcutta was fraught with difficulty. It took three attempts and was an unintended consequence of the Company's most ill-judged war, also known as 'Child's War' (1686-90), against the Moghul Empire when under its most aggressive and intolerant ruler, the Emperor Aurangzeb (1658-1707).

In 1686, at the instigation of Sir Josiah Child, a major stockholder and influential director, a Company fleet was sent from England with instructions to 'enter into war with the

Moghul'. This was an extraordinary proposition given the balance of forces but the decision had been taken after a prolonged and fruitless negotiation with the nawab of Bengal over trading privileges. Child seems to have imagined that the Company could be at war with the Moghul province of Bengal in the east while simultaneously trading peacefully from Moghul-ruled Bombay and Surat on the west coast. As a Captain William Hamilton reported: 'By what rule of policy could Sir Josiah Child … think to rob, murder and destroy the Moghul's subjects in one part of his dominions and the Company to enforce free trade in other parts? Or how could he expect that he [the Moghul] would stand neuter?' In any case, as if to ensure a hostile reaction in all parts of the Moghul Empire, once the English fleet arrived at Surat it proceeded to harass Moghul shipping so that Bombay soon came under Moghul pressure. Meanwhile two ships carrying a company of infantry sailed on for Bengal.

The two ships arrived at the mouth of the River Hooghly in the autumn of 1686. Fortunately, no one had informed the Nawab of Bengal that the British were at war with him, although, given recent tensions, he had moved several thousand troops to the town of Hooghly as a precaution before the British ships arrived, Hooghly being the site of the senior Company trading post in Bengal at that time. With exceptional good manners, this Moghul force allowed the company of infantry to disembark from the two English ships once they arrived and allowed the English soldiers to join their British fellows in the settlement. There followed a few weeks of uneasy truce, until 28 October 1686 when three British soldiers out shopping in the bazaar were 'beate, cut, and carried prisoner' to the Moghul governor, whereupon the British reacted ferociously: one British soldier was killed in the fighting which ensued and sixty of the Moghul government forces.

Despite this small victory, the British forces at Hooghly were still overwhelmingly outnumbered. Job Charnock, British leader in

Bengal, loaded all the Company's stores into the two ships and some other vessels, evacuated the town and sailed downriver. He landed off a long deep stretch of water, the highest point upriver that ocean-going ships could reach. It was a strategic choice. There was a high mud rise on its eastern bank and there he pitched camp by a 'low, swampy village of scattered huts'. He called it 'Chuttanutteea' after the village of Sutanati, one of three villages within the bounds of early Calcutta, another being the village of Kalighat, which gave the town its name.

After a period of fruitless negotiation with the Nawab's representatives during the winter of 1686/7, Charnock, fearing that a Moghul army was being raised against him, went on a threatening rampage. He took ship yet again and burned down the town of Balasore on the coast then pitched camp at Hijili, the last island on the Hooghly estuary before it spills into the Bay of Bengal. Enraged, the Nawab ordered an army to follow and there followed a month-long stand-off. It was now May 1687, the hottest, most humid, month of the year and half the British force died of fever. On 28 May, the Moghuls attacked; the British managed to hold them off although only just. Charnock now faced a choice between evacuation or surrender. If he had been more a religious man – he had married a Hindu widow so this was in question[95] – he might have suspected divine intervention in what followed because, four days later, the annual Company fleet from England arrived at the mouth of the river and the tables were turned. After a brief foray by seventy sailors, the Moghuls raised a flag of truce and in the subsequent negotiations the Company's trading rights were secured. Charnock was granted permission to choose a fortified site for the Company's factory in Bengal.

---

95 Keay, John (1991): *The Honourable Company*: p151: Charncok is said to have saved her from suttee.

Three months later, the British were back at Sutanati and temporary shelters were again being built along the mud ridge above the river.

But then, in October 1688, the British position changed yet again. A new agent, William Heath, arrived aboard the *Defence* with instructions from the Directors to take over from Charnock. Heath insisted that the British decamp to the Chittagong river, in modern Burma, and form an alliance against the Moghul Empire with the Arrakan pirates based there. Charnock and his men had no choice but to pack their bags and leave with Heath but, having arrived in Chittagong, Heath found that the Burmese rajah had no interest in an alliance with him so he then sailed for Madras. Forty years trade in Bengal appeared to have come to an end.

But it had not. The next saviour of the British in Bengal was unexpected. On the west coast, Emperor Aurangzeb forced humiliating terms of surrender on the Company's men at Bombay and Surat but Child's War had always been absurd and for Aurangzeb 'the Company was still a mere flea on the back of his imperial elephant'.[96] Aurangzeb valued the customs dues paid by British and other European merchants, indeed it was a very important source of income for him. In what could almost be described as an act of irony, and in return for the abject submission of the British, he was pleased to restore their trading rights. Suddenly there was no impediment to a British return to Bengal and the 'Bengal gentlemen' set sail from Madras (1690). At the mouth of the Hooghly they transferred to sloops and Job Charnock and thirty troops reached Sutanati shortly after, on 24 August, 'the rain falling day and night'. All traces of their former settlement were gone but they set to work rebuilding - and this time they had come to stay.

---

[96] Keay, John (1991): *The Honourable Company*: p146.

The next four to five years of Calcutta were precarious but they provided an opportunity. In 1695, Hooghly was captured by rebels against Nawab Ibrahim Khan. The rebels then moved against Calcutta and the British requested permission to defend themselves. Permission was given but not permission to build a fort - they started work on fortifications anyway that very night, using mortar brought from Madras. Their new fort dominated the high mudbank where Sutanati had once stood and it was completed in 1701, named 'Fort William' after King William III.

Calcutta grew to be considerably wealthier than Madras because its Bengal hinterland was then one of the largest economies in the world. Before its foundation, the richest merchant families in the region were the Seths and Basacks, merchants of yarn and cloth at Sutanati, and these families benefited from the arrival of the British and were significant contributors towards the development of the town. This alliance between wealthy Hindus and the British, both formally excluded from administrative power in the late Moghul empire, was a feature of the development of Calcutta, witness the alliance between Joseph Fowke and Maharajah Nuncomar in 1775 (*see* pages 109-115).

From its foundation in 1790, Calcutta attracted Indian and European merchants and skilled tradesmen, drawn by its relative security and religious toleration. Like Madras, Calcutta was a haven in turbulent times. It developed its own 'White Town', mostly to the north of the Fort, and a 'Black Town' in the Sutanati area. However, as the eighteenth century progressed, the British became over-confident and neglected the maintenance of Fort William. They began to abuse their trading privileges thereby denying the government of Bengal the customs duties which were a central contribution to its revenues. Calcutta became in some Indian eyes, a place of ill repute and a large class of 'low Europeans' or 'European vagabonds' lowered its standing. Such men might be former soldiers turned inn-keepers, or they might be servants or sailors but they were not figures of authority; indeed there was contempt for law and authority among this group and fighting and drunkenness were rife. The lawlessness was exacerbated because for many years the worst punishment available for English wrong-doers was deportation back to England. There was no capital punishment in Calcutta until towards the end of the century.

Things came to a head in in 1756 when Nawab Siraj-ud-Daulah, infuriated by British avoidance of tax and customs dues, finally attacked. By that time, due to penny-pinching by the Directors, Fort William was 'more like a deserted ruined Moorish fort than any place in the possession of Europeans' and it was sacked. The town was captured and Sophia Holland, Joseph Fowke's sister, by then a widow, escaped a mere day before the fall of the settlement.[97] There followed the infamous Black Hole of Calcutta, when forty-three British prisoners died of heat exhaustion or suffocation. The stage was set for Robert Clive's rescue mission from Madras and his subsequent victory at the Battle of Plassey, with John Walsh as his paymaster and others in his train.

---

[97] Eileen and Harry Green, *The Fowkes of Boughrood Castle,* p 7.

# 7. Francis, Arthur and Margaret

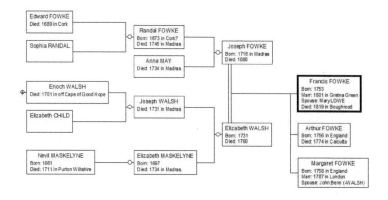

rancis Fowke, John Walsh's nephew and elder son of Joseph Fowke, was born on 28th October 1753, the same month that the recently married Clives returned from India following Clive's triumph at Arcot. Joseph wrote to John Walsh from London:

> *I have domestic satisfactions which fall to the share of very few … If I had been much richer I much question if I could have been much happier … Betsy is very well and perfectly recovered from her lying in, except her sight, which is still weak, and prevents her writing to you. You may be assured nothing else would. I designed making you a Godfather to our little boy, but your sister told me you were averse to such a charge. His name is Francis and he was born 28th October last, is an uncommon*

*lusty boy and looks as if he did not belong to either of us, and begins to make a general fool of his mother.*[98]

The Fowkes lived relatively moderately on around £1,200-1,500 per year. Their immediate circle consisted of Joseph's brothers, Edward in London and Francis at Malmesbury in Wiltshire; also the Clives and the Hollands (Sophia Holland was Joseph's younger sister); also Jenny Kelsall/Lathom (the third of the three cousins - Margaret Maskelyne/Clive, Elizabeth Walsh/Fowke and Jenny – who had been brought up by the Maskelyne aunts, Jane and Sarah, in Wiltshire).

Elizabeth Fowke enjoyed motherhood. Her letters to the aunts are full of references to her children, first Francis, then Arthur, born 1756. Her health was fragile however and already giving cause for concern before she became pregnant with her third child, Margaret. Margaret was born on 13 July 1758 and baptised at Hanover Square in London. Liz's letters describe her joy at the birth but the shadows of ill health and of Joseph's increasing interest in cards cast a shadow:

*… the day before yesterday I dined with Sir John Chapman, an acquaintance Mr Fowke picked up at the card table where he is pretty much taken up in the evening … we shall come to town in about a month…*[99]

John Walsh returned from India in 1759, as we have seen, and set about the building of Warfield Park. There followed the bitter row between him and Joseph in which Liz took her husband's side. Joseph's letters were typically severe:

---

[98] Eur D456: Correspondence of the Fowke, Benn, Walsh and Maskelyne familes, Vol. 4, p. 35: Joseph Fowke to John Walsh, 20 January 1754.

[99] Eur D456: Correspondence of the Fowke, Benn, Walsh and Maskelyne familes, Vol. 2, p 62: Elizabeth Fowke to aunts Jane and Sarah Masquelyne, Tunbridge Wells, 25 July 1759.

*Sir ... calculate exactly what Money has been employed upon your Account and charge me the interest for the difference. I will most willingly give up all my commission to be released from the Plague your Affairs have given me – [Humble servant etc].*[100]

Joseph returned a gift of £10,000 to Walsh, which constituted a significant proportion of his capital. Then Liz died - a year after her brother's return from India. She left her three children motherless but her death brought about a reconciliation between Joseph and Walsh, even though Joseph claimed that her last words were an instruction that he 'should never receive a shilling from my brother' – which seems unlikely because she was, by all accounts, a kind and entertaining person, as Margaret Clive would testify in a letter to her niece Margaret Maskelyne, written many years later in 1806 (The reference to astronomy is typical.):

*... I love my cousins full well, Walshes, Stracheys, and always regret Mrs Fowke's bright meridien has been so dimmed by unfortunate circumstances ... that lovely Globe Sir John Walsh so kindly gave me .. I doat on my globe.*[101]

Joseph went to pieces, if he was not in pieces already. He gambled away what was left of his fortune and, although he remained in England until 1771, John Walsh became the effective protector of Joseph's children. The two boys were sent first to a small private school and then to Cheam, now in the southern suburbs of London, at Walsh's expense. From 1755, the headmaster was the author and artist William Gilpin. The boys were fortunate because Gilpin was an enlightened educationalist. There were fines rather than corporal punishment and the boys were encouraged to garden

---

[100] Eur D456: Correspondence of the Fowke, Benn, Walsh and Maskelyne familes, Vol. 4, ps 69/70: Joseph Fowke to John Walsh, 3 April 1760.

[101] Mss Eur: Vol. 1, Part 3 *P287*: Margaret Clive to her niece Margaret Masquelyne, Oakley Park Easter Day 1806.

and to keep 'in-school' shops. Gilpin's aim was to encourage 'uprightness and utility' and a 'miniature of the world they were afterwards to enter' - although in Francis he may also have encouraged a certain disdain for authority. Gilpin described Francis as 'the cleverest of all his pupils' although, judging by the correspondence, Arthur was equally clever. Also at Cheam were their cousins John and Edward Holland. Edward 'cherished and protected' Arthur when he was a new boy.

Meanwhile Margaret began her strange, peripatetic childhood, shared between John Walsh at Warfield and Chesterfield Street and, to a lesser extent, under the kindly eyes of Lady Clive at Berkley Square or Walcot in Shropshire and Jenny Kelsall/Lathom. Clive liked to put Margaret on his knee then get her to recite any naughty words she had learned at school. This letter from Lady Clive at Walcot Hall in Shropshire gives a flavour of her life at that time:

> *My dear Miss Fowke,*
> *It would have given me much pleasure to have heard from my dear Miss Fowke, but as I did not make it a request this summer, she has not thought it a duty to make me so happy. I wish my good girl had of her own free will written to me, but I am now coming to town and shall have the pleasure of seeing her … I know it will be very agreeable to you to hear that Lord Clive has enjoyed good health at Walcot … My dear Peggy our happiness has been somewhat interrupted by the loss of some relations of Lord Clive and we have felt much for our poor sisters … Miss Ducarel is well & with your relations here, joins in best wishes to you & your brothers; please accept of Lord Clive's, but thank him for them in London. I have left my little girls a great while & am returning to them with great willingness … my boy Bob is but a little shrymp but very lively and can prattle a little; you shall hear him Peggy. I am my*

*dear Miss Fowke your very affectionate Friend & Godmother M Clive*[102]

*...all my girls remember you, & ask affectionately after you. Pray accept their love & good wishes. Lord Clive and Miss Ducarel desire the same to you. I dearly loved your mother & am tenderly attached to you ...*[103]

These eminent relatives took a kindly interest in Margaret's development and she seems to have picked up much of her education by roaming their libraries although paid teachers and others did much of the day-to-day caring. She was looked after in Reading (near to Warfield) and sometimes in Bath, firstly by a Mrs Kitchens, who was a good pianist[104] helped by a Mrs Ledien, then by a Mrs Hawkin and Mrs Wheelock when she was allowed to practise dancing as well as music. Walsh kept an eye:

*If Mrs Kitchin or Mrs Ledien be so good ... they will please to let you practise Dancing and Musick should Bath furnish any masters they approve, but always in their company ...*[105]

It was not a happy childhood and she must have looked forward to holidays spent with her elder brothers. Joseph continued to take an interest in his daughter but from afar and all three children inherited from their father a passionate interest in music. Margaret also became interested in mathematics. Her sense of insecurity cannot have been helped when, in 1769 when she was eleven, Joseph had a daughter, Sophia, by a young woman called Lavinia or 'Kitty' Treacher, whom he had the decency to marry the

---

102 Mss Eur Vol. 8, p78: Lady Clive to Margaret Fowke, Walcot, 25 November, 1771.

103 Eur D456: Correspondence of the Fowke, Benn, Walsh and Maskelyne familes, Vol. 8, p79: Lady Clive to Margaret Fowke, Oakley Park, 1771.

104 Woodfield, Ian (2000): Music of the Raj: p83.

105 Mss Eur, Handlists, Kaye, 10R lists 308, p80: John Walsh to Margaret Fowke, 25 February 1772.

following year (1ˢᵗ September 1770). To add insult to injury, in 1770 he had another daughter, Louisa, so he now had another family to look after even though his original children were still being cared for by John Walsh. Francis, Arthur and Margaret never accepted their half-sisters as equals, perhaps from resentment at their father's fecklessness although snobbery came into it also. Arthur wrote to Margaret shortly before accompanying John Walsh to Brittany:

> *I think it was improper in my Father to make mention of his wife to us; but he does not seem to think his conduct in marrying this woman indiscreet, nor to know that the thought of such a mother in law must be disagreeable to us …*[106]

Margaret reacted badly. She was unhappy at Mrs Kitchens in Reading and then with Mrs Hawkins. It seems that at Mrs Hawkin's she was to some extent constrained against her will; as Francis wrote later.[107]

> *I know very well the constant strain you were under and that it was impossible for you to open your mind freely to me … old Mrs Hawkins is a strange mortal.*

Margaret's response was unusual. In 1773 she wrote a series of anonymous letters to herself and claimed that she had been accosted and robbed by a masked man who set fire to her room. Modern psychologists would give her behaviour serious consideration. It was acry for help. At first she was believed. Her uncle Edward described the incident to Francis:

---

[106] Mss Eur, Handlists, Kaye, 1OR lists 308, p80: Arthur Fowke to his sister Margaret, Chesterfield Street, April 1772.

[107] Mss Eur, Handlists, Kaye, 1OR lists 308, p67.

*Your sister Peggy had her watch taken from her at Noonday over the Rales at Mrs Hawkins by a man just dismounted, mask'd and with a pistol in his hand ...*[108]

It became apparent that the masked man was a fabrication and there was much disapproval, including from Margaret Clive. John Walsh, perhaps more aware of the emotional neglect that Margaret had endured than was Margaret Clive, arranged for his niece to be looked after in her brother Francis's apartment at Warfield Park, the start of a further unhappy interlude in her life. Her uncle Edward Fowke wrote to Francis:

*Peggy has for some months past occupied your old apartments at Warfield ... Your sister's idle nonsensical schemes may be told two ways: one very bad and the best footing it could be put would be insanity. But Mrs Hawkins relates it in a much more favourable light – that she was afraid of her uncle which first put her on scheming and writing those nonsensical letters ... she first broke some of the windows in her room and sett fire to some of the things ... You may suppose Mr Walsh has made her suffer severely for such bad behaviour – however it is but justice to say his behaviour is affectionate forgiving & good to her ...*[109]

Walsh had arranged for Francis, then aged twenty, to sign up as a writer for the East India Company and Francis sailed in 1773, the year of Margaret's protest. The three siblings were always very close and perhaps his departure, or impending departure, contributed to her breakdown. The following year, Walsh arranged for Arthur to follow his brother and settled £150 per year on each of the three siblings.

---

[108] Mss Eur, Handlists, Kaye, 10R lists 308, p71: abstract of letter from Edward Fowke to his nephew Francis Fowke, Hawley, 24 May ,1773.

[109] Minor Collections Fowke Mss 20-44, p.72: abstract of letter from Edward Fowke to his nephew Francis Fowke, Curzon Street, 29 March 1774.

Arthur only just made it to India. In a letter written at False Bay, 24 July 1775, he describes himself 'seized with a spitting of blood, eat very little of anything & abstain wholly from animal food'. He died shortly after his arrival in Madras. 'He was very handsome'.[110]

Two years later, Margaret embarked at Gravesend after spending seven weeks with Margaret Clive at Oakley Park in Shropshire.[111] She was eighteen and her uncle Edward Fowke announced her departure in a letter to Francis who was by then the Company's Resident (= representative) at Benares:

*Your sister goes out now, I suppose, to get her a husband which she has not beauty or fortune enough to get here ... Your sisters Sophy and Loui went to school at Cirencester the 30th inst.[112]*

Margaret was eager to free herself of John Walsh's generous but autocratic control and she longed to join her brother because the only close family these three, now two, siblings had had during their childhood was each other. She was also re-joining her father Joseph who had returned to India and was now widowed for the second time. Joseph had sailed with Kitty Treacher in 1771, leaving their two daughters, Sophia and Louisa, in the care of his younger brother Francis in Malmesbury. Francis never married and seems to have adopted a kindly attitude towards the girls. He was a 'mild, amiable and agreeable man, a musician, well-read and a linguist ... he had bad health and was "ridden to death" by a hobby involving the invention of a universal language in which all books were to be written'.[113] He sent Sophia and Louisa

---

[110] Mss Eur 032, *Memoir of Margaret Elizabeth Benn-Walsh (nee Fowke)*, by her son John Benn-Walsh.

[111] Eur D456: Correspondence of the Fowke, Benn, Walsh and Maskelyne familes, Vol. 30, p 75: Margaret Fowke to her brother Francis, Chesterfield Street 7 December 1775.

[112] Mss Eur, Handlists, Mss Eur Kaye, 10R lists 308, p 75 abstract of letter from Edward Fowke to his nephew Francis, Curzon Street, 22 November 1775.

[113] *Fowke Family Tree*, Ray Fowke p.475.

to the school in Cirencester referred to in Edward Fowke's letter, where Margaret Clive had once been educated. Kitty Treacher had died alone on the island of St Helena in 1774, on her way home to be reunited with her daughters, life in India with Joseph having perhaps proved too difficult.

Eighteen-year-old Margaret Fowke sailed in the new year of 1776 on the *Camden* with a Miss Pybus, daughter of a friend of the Clives and rather less conscientious. During the voyage Margaret studiously read Pope's *Homer* and began Virgil's *Aenias* 'which I have borrowed, and study arithmetic, French and geography'; Miss Pybus gave 'encouragement' to a cadet and had to be spoken to by Captain Reddel. The girls carried letters of introduction, vital for new arrivals to India. This was from Lady Clive to Mrs Casamajor, a prominent Madras citizen:

> *I have lately drank a large draught of Sorrow, and am now humbling myself under this severe stroke … I find myself at this time called upon to render a service to a young relation of mine, the child of the amiable Mrs Fowke, whom you and I so entirely loved and respected … Miss Fowke takes her passage on Captain Reddel's ship…[114]*

On arrival in Calcutta, Margaret had expected to stay with her aunt, Mrs Sophia Holland (Joseph Fowke's sister), but Sophia died before she got there and Margaret was obliged to find lodgings with a Mrs Lacam, both her father and her brother being then at Benares. It was several months before father and brother were forced to leave Benares and the remains of the family were finally reunited in Calcutta, a poignant occasion with both a mother and a brother dead – although so too was Kitty Treacher, which made things easier.

---

[114] EUR, Kaye, Minor Collections Mss Eur, Handlists, p 82: abstract of letter from Lady Clive to Mrs Casamajor, Oakley Park, 7 December, 1775.

1. Fort St. George, Madras circa 1754.

2. Randal's memorial stone with inscription by
Joseph, St Mary's, Madras.

3. Memorial stones, St Mary's, Madras.

4. Fort Marlborough, Bencoolen, Sumatra.

5. Masula boats.

6. Fort St. David, Tamil Nadu.

7. Lieut. Col. John Walsh MP, 1781, pastel by Sharpless of Bath.

8. Warfield Park, Bracknell, Berkshire.

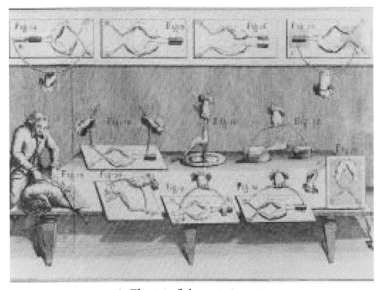

9. Electric fish experiment.

10. Calcutta.

11. John Clavering, 1722-77.

12. Philip Francis, 1740-1818, by Lonsdale.

13. Warren Hastings, 1732-1818, by Joshua Reynolds.

14. Elijah Impey, 1732-1809.

15. George Monson, 1730-76.

16. Robert Chambers, 1737-1803.

17. The Old Court House, Calcutta.

18. Turban of Nuncomar, Victoria Memorial Museum.

19. Budgerow.

20. Benares.

21. Chait Singh's house, Benares, by William Daniels.

22. Opium fleet on the Ganges around 1790.

23. Mary Lowe, 1769-1847.

24. Octagon House, Wimbledon, now demolished.

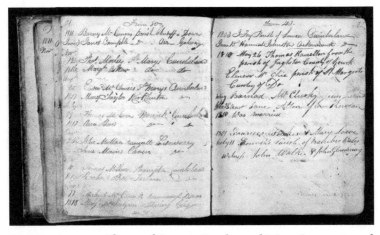

25. Marriage certificate of Francis Fowke and Mary Lowe, signed at Gretna Green.

27. Close up of marriage certificate.

28. Boughrood Castle, Radnorshire.

# 8. Joseph again

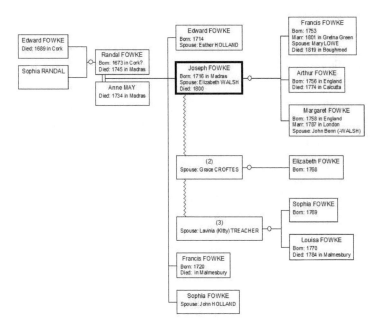

A fter Liz Walsh/Fowke died in 1760, family tradition has it that Joseph Fowke went rapidly downhill, that he gambled away his fortune and was obliged to return to India as a free merchant in order to build a new one. In fact his ill fortune had begun before her death. As we have seen, he had quarrelled bitterly with brother-in-law John Walsh after Walsh's return from

India in 1759 and had repaid him £10,000, a considerable sum. His 'passion for play' now got the better of him– as far as we can tell.[115] The problem with trying to reconstruct Joseph's character from his many surviving letters is that as well as being very good, if difficult, company, he habitually overstated things. A tall, thin man with dark hair and grey eyes, subject to uncontrollable fits of anger who was passionately interested in music and in the events of his day, he got things wrong repeatedly but was also principled, critical of wrong doing in others and very capable of affection.

The death of Liz seems to have undermined him in more ways than one. In 1768 he had a daughter, Elizabeth, by a woman called Grace Crofts before marrying 'Kitty' Treacher following the birth of their daughter Sophia. When their second daughter, Louisa, was on the way he wrote to Robert Clive asking for assistance with his return to India, because he needed to go back there to recoup his fortune. It must have been a difficult letter to write given Margaret Clive's resentment over the poor hand her beloved cousin Liz Walsh/Fowke had been dealt when she married Joseph. At first he asked Clive to help him find employment with the East India Company, indeed to help him find a senior position. The obsequiousness must have been difficult:

*When unavoidable misfortunes come upon us we receive consolation from the reflection that they were unavoidable, but when they happen to us by our own folly, the silent reproaches of our friends are sharpened by a conviction of their propriety. I shall therefore offer nothing in justification of my conduct, but leave my reputation to the mercy of the world … nor shou'd I have open'd this far, except with a view of removing prejudices you may have unjustly conceived against me, as I have long since remark'd a coolness in your lordship which I have been utterly at a loss*

[115] Eur D456: Correspondence of the Fowke, Benn, Walsh and Maskelyne familes, Vol. 6, p 177: Robert Clive to Luke Serafton, 2 December 1770.

*to account for … If you Lordship should encourage my daring attempt for a government …'[116]*

When Clive proved unhelpful, it was necessary to put a gloss on the gambling and on his marriage to a much younger woman:

*… I allow that Play is a vice, and that I have been guilty of it in several parts of my life; it is a distemper that has run in the blood of my family, my father who was under the influence of the same passion before me … I allow that I have been strongly and tenderly attached – in appearance perhaps viciously so at my time of life and in my circumstances, but I will not allow more than the appearance, unless it should be thought a vice to rescue from the foul hands of contagion injured innocence, oppress'd honour and the most exalted virtues that ever adorned the soul of a woman … I blush not, my Lord, to say … that I have prevented a most fair flower from perishing among weeds.*[117]

Clive did his best but he was wracked by illness and depression. Lady Clive wrote in desperation to Walsh:

*4 O'clock Shrewsbury morn & afternoon*
*What can I say? So many changes! An interval of ease,& then so great an opposition of spirits seizes my poor Lord Clive, that his miserable family know not what to do … I do not believe Lord Clive in danger, notwithstanding, were it the first time, my brain would be destroyed by hearing him protest he wishes for death and his sufferings are beyond human bearing.*[118]

---

[116] Eur D456: Correspondence of the Fowke, Benn, Walsh and Maskelyne familes, Vol. 6, p 168/9: Joseph Fowke to Robert Clive, Hanover Square, London.

[117] Eur D456: Correspondence of the Fowke, Benn, Walsh and Maskelyne familes, Vol. 6, p 170: Joseph Fowke to Robert Clive, Hanover Square, 9 Sept 1770.

[118] Eur D456: Correspondence of the Fowke, Benn, Walsh and Maskelyne familes, Vols 8/9, p 24: Margaret Clive to John Walsh, Sept 1770.

By December 1770 Clive was well enough to write somewhat ambivalent letters of introduction for Joseph to take with him both for Madras and Calcutta.

> *I need not trouble you with the history of Jos. Fowke – you know his passion for play ... I could not refuse him letters of introduction to my friends in India, & as I have always understood him to be a man of principle and sense, tho' not common sense, I can not help wishing you would give him all the assistance in your power to rescue him from his present state of distress ...[119]*
>
> *The bearer of this, Mr Fowke, is an unhappy and imprudent man but his honour and integrity stand unimpeached and his abilities are above the common level ... putting him the way to recover a competency which he once enjoyed. As the Diamond trade in Bengal is yet in its infancy I doubt not that Mr Fowke will have an eye towards it. He has much experience in the branch of business .. I hope that he will merit your protection ...[120]*

As we have seen, in 1771 Joseph returned to India with Kitty Treacher as a 'free merchant' in the diamond trade, leaving their daughters Sophia and Louisa in the care of Joseph's bachelor brother Francis in Malmesbury. A 'free merchant' meant that he was not a servant of the Company and would have to make his fortune by himself without that additional status and security. He was in Madras by August of that year and received a frosty welcome, as he reported to Clive:

> *My Lord, I arrived here the 25 ... Mr Duprée took not the least notice of your letter of recommendation to me. He invited me twice to his house,*

---

[119] Eur D456: Correspondence of the Fowke, Benn, Walsh and Maskelyne familes, Vol. 6, p 177: Robert Clive to Luke Serafton, 2 December 1770.

[120] Eur D456: Correspondence of the Fowke, Benn, Walsh and Maskelyne familes, Vol. 6, p. 181: Robert Clive to John Cartier, Berkley Square, 28 January 1771.

*and when I came there said not a word to me – his behaviour was perfectly refrigerating and I could not at last help turning my back on him … I don't know what opinion others may entertain of this gentleman but mine is that his talents for affairs are not superior to the specimen he has given of his address … Mr Hastings polite but couldn't help … I am left in turbulent times to push my way unaided as I can … I set sail this evening for Bengal.[121]*

So he moved on to Calcutta whence he wrote again to Clive, describing his reception in Madras as reason for the move:

*My Lord … he [Duprée] was cold, phlegmatick and unfeeling, partly perhaps from his own make and constitution and partly perhaps from a consciousness of a want of those powers necessary to command, which were to be made up in him by a formal parade, the last paltry defence of mean pride and childish … as everybody in general is eager to throw their commissions into my hands, notwithstanding Lamotte remains a rival, so that I am likely to be supplied further with money than with diamonds.[122]*

The 1769-73 Bengal famine, one of the darkest episodes of British power in India, was only recently over and Calcutta also proved to be less than welcoming even if some 'commissions' were forthcoming. He left and travelled up-river to Benares (Varenasi), now part of the modern Indian province of Uttar Pradesh but then a semi-independent kingdom since it was only nominally subject to the Nawab (Moghul governor) of Oudh (modern Awadh) to the north, now also a region of Uttar Pradesh. Joseph had landed

---

[121] Eur D456: Correspondence of the Fowke, Benn, Walsh and Maskelyne familes, Vol. 6, p 188: Joseph Fowke to Robert Clive, Fort St George, 25 August 1771.

[122] Eur D456: Correspondence of the Fowke, Benn, Walsh and Maskelyne familes, Vol. 6, p 188: Joseph Fowke to Robert Clive, Calcutta 15 November 1771.

among a nest of vipers. The British had rung various trading privileges out of the then Rajah of Benares in 1765 and a number of unscrupulous British traders had set up shop there, avoiding the local taxes and irritating the local authorities who were powerless to control them. The last thing these traders wanted was competition from an experienced man such as Joseph and they set out to deny him access, supported by the hostile influence of the Commander of the Company's Bengal troops, General Robert Barker, who incidentally was also a competitor in the diamond trade. After weeks of trying, Joseph eventually decided to return to Calcutta - until persuaded to stay by Rajah Chait Singh's men who came after him in a boat. His status as a man who had once been second in council in Madras, who had negotiated for the governorship of Bengal and who claimed friendship with Clive must have played its part:

*My Lord, I arrived the 7th and have been in my Badgerow ever since with all my family, exposed to the hurricanes and burning hot sands for want of a house which the rajah would not give any order for – I set sail back to Calcutta the 13th and the Rajah's people overtook me the 14th and insisted very earnestly upon my return, excusing the slight upon me by very frivolous apologies. It became clear to me at last that Captain Smith had a hand in the indignities which were shown me. General Barker too, I know, has been always averse to my settling here under any other character than that of a diamond factor by which I might perhaps, whilst Motte was on the spot, gain £500 a year. I envy not these gentlemen the glorious triumph of opposing the progress and defeating the struggles of a ruin'd man reduc'd to the utmost farthing. In this first act however of malevolence, I think I have gotten the better of my enemy for the Rajah [Chait Singh] met me upon my return, apologized for the incivility, and by his orders I enter this day into a good house. Middleton has set his face likewise against me, so that these men to whom I was recommended have turned out my fiercest opponents –*

*when will my evils end! – They may break my heart but they will never bend it.*

*I am my lord etc…*[123]

By then, he had been living on his river boat or 'budgerow' for several months and it was small wonder that Kitty Treacher eventually left him to return to England. However, from March 1772, with Rajah Chait Singh's support, things began to look up. He was able to start trading in diamonds and he had a decent house to live in. By July he had formed a partnership with Thomas Motte, who was a friend of Warren Hastings by then Governor of Bengal. Hastings had been appointed Governor in 1771 and had been helpful to Joseph, although Joseph's attitude was lukewarm:

*My Lord, Hastings professed friendship but has done nothing – I don't think nature has given to Hastings any executive powers, and so far I can most freely forgive him, but some doubt hangs upon my mind of his Insincerity …*[124]*'*

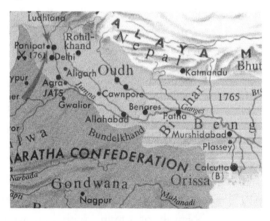

[123] Eur D456: Correspondence of the Fowke, Benn, Walsh and Maskelyne families, Vol. 6, p 194: Joseph Fowke to Robert Clive, Benares, 13 March 1772.

[124] Eur D456: Correspondence of the Fowke, Benn, Walsh and Maskelyne families, Vol. 6, p 198: Joseph Fowke to Robert Clive, Benares, 15 March 1773.

When Joseph arrived in Benares, the political and military situation in northern India was far from stable. Benares and Oudh were threatened by the Marathas, a confederation of warlike Hindu states that controlled most of central India, and the Moghul Emperor Shah Alam was almost powerless in Delhi under Maratha control. In 1772, Shah Alam was forced to cede Allahabad and Kora, both near to Oudh and Benares, to the Marathas bringing them to the southern banks of the Ganges where they could lurk, threatening Oudh. Shuja-ud-Daulah, the Nawab of Oudh, and General Barker (without Hastings's participation) formed an alliance with the Rohillas for additional support against this threat because the Rohillas were also threatened. They were Pathan Afghans from the region of Kandahar, who had seized control of an area to the north of Delhi. They were no angels; after the Battle of Panipat of 1761 they had slaughtered some 40,000 defenceless Maratha prisoners so they had every reason to fear Maratha vengeance. The treaty that Shuja-ud-Daulah and General Barker signed with the Rohillas stated that Oudh with a British army would come to the defence of the Rohillas in return for forty lacs of rupees (approximately 400,000 rupees) to be paid to Oudh by the Rohillas, a sum that Siraj-ud-Daulah saw as owing to him in any case due to previous Rohilla exactions.

The Rohillas were unreliable. By March, they were still refusing to pay. Hastings decided that the best policy for the Company was help Oudh to subdue the Rohillas so that Oudh could form a strong, defensible buffer state against the Mahrattas along the course of the central Ganges. On 24 June 1773, Hastings left Calcutta for Benares to negotiate a new treaty along these lines with Siraj-ud-Daulah, the Nawab of Oudh. With him were fellow members of the Calcutta Council, George Vansittart and George Lambert. They made slow progress upriver, held back by 'foul winds, violent currents and separation of our fleet' and did not reach Benares, where Joseph was still resident, until 19th August. It had taken fifty-six days to travel 420 miles. There followed two weeks of strenuous haggling with Siraj-ud-Daulah.

The result was the Treaty of Benares. Under its terms Allahabad and Kora were 'returned' to Oudh, whether the Emperor in Delhi agreed or not, and the East India Company agreed to support Oudh *against* the Rohillas in return for a large cash payment. In addition, the Company confirmed the status of Chait Singh, as Raja of Benares and all the British merchants then resident in the city were ordered to leave - with the exception of Joseph Fowke, Thomas Motte and one other.[125]

Hastings was back in Calcutta by October and Siraj-ud-Daulah, now confident of British support, lost little time in launching an attack on the Rohillas. He now had British forces at his disposal. The Rohillas resisted but they were no match for trained European troops. They were defeated by Colonel Alexander Champion at the Battle of Miranpur Katra on 23 April 1774.

On the surface things were more secure, but back in Benares, Joseph was still struggling, despite his privileged position as one of only three British traders in the city:

*My Lord,*

*I am not, nor do I see that I am likely to be, one six pence the better for the friendship of any man in India. I am condemned to suffer a painful exile and live like a dog upon the small pittance of 2 ½% commission on the purchase of diamonds without any earthly advantage besides ... If fortune does not throw something better in my way, I propose leaving India in November 1775 with the reputation of having gained the least money of any man who has inhabited these regions for ten years past above the rank of butcher.[126]*

---

[125] Feiling, Keith (1966): *Warren Hastings*: p 115.

[126] Eur D456: Correspondence of the Fowke, Benn, Walsh and Maskelyne familes, Vol. 6, p 200: Joseph Fowke to Robert Clive, Benares, 28 September 1773.

Joseph was perhaps also troubled by a discontented or sickly Kitty Treacher who would soon be on her way home. She was no doubt missing her two daughters, still in the care of Joseph's brother Francis in Malmesbury, and life with Joseph had perhaps not worked out quite as she had been led to anticipate. She embarked late in 1773 and Joseph probably returned to Calcutta with her to see her onto her ship. Or perhaps they planned be reunited in England and it was simply that she went first, impatient to see her daughters. In any case, he had another reason to leave Benares:

> My Lord,
>
> I write this to acquaint you I have been driven from Benares. Mr Motte supported by Mr Hastings were too powerful for me to withstand … I have been here six weeks and had the honour of receiving one invitation from Mr Hastings. It is a most corrupted air that I breathe here. It agrees ill with my constitution. I have not received a single favour from anyone in India and, starving as I am, there are few I would choose to receive. I was not made for the times, the times were not made for me, I can't say which …[127]

Kitty died on St Helena in 1774 while on the passage home and Francis, Joseph's son, almost passed her on the high sea coming out from England. He had at last managed to escape John Walsh's autocratic care and had embarked for India in 1773, being followed the next year by his brother Arthur, who died shortly after landing in 1775. It was a time of deaths: there was Kitty, then Clive who died in November 1774, probably suicide, then Arthur.

Joseph stayed on in Calcutta where he was joined by Francis and, despite the tenor of his letters to Clive, he seems to have made some money from trading in diamonds at this time. Things were never straightforward with Joseph however. He had taken strongly

---

[127] Eur D456: Correspondence of the Fowke, Benn, Walsh and Maskelyne familes, Vol. 7, p 202: Joseph Fowke to Robert Clive, Calcutta, 22 March 1774.

against Warren Hastings and began to search for a means to remove him from office.

Help was on its way. By 1772/3, popular opinion in Britain had swung strongly against the Company because of the disaster of the Bengal Famine, during which a third of the population died, and from concern at a private company acquiring such power with so little responsibility. The conspicuous wealth of returning 'nabobs' was also offensive. In addition the Company was in financial trouble due to its military adventures and the cost of administering its enlarged territories subsequent to Clive's victory at Plassey. On 19 June 1773, Parliament passed the Regulating Act: in return for a loan from the government of £1.4 million, the Company agreed to accept a Governor General appointed by Parliament with authority over all the Company's interests in India, thus uniting Madras, Bombay and Calcutta under a single head for the first time. Warren Hastings was appointed to this post, a sensible choice: he had been in India since 1750 and had a reputation for courage and diligence. He spoke both Urdu and Farsi and took a great interest in Indian affairs and culture.

If Warren Hastings had been given complete authority, the Company's affairs in India might have gone relatively smoothly from this point but in addition to the appointment of a Governor General, the Regulating Act also called for a new Supreme Court and for the appointment of three councillors whose job was to oversee the Governor General on behalf of Parliament. It was in the inherent tension in the roles of Hastings as Governor General and these three councillors, the 'Triumphirate' comprising Philip Francis, General Clavering and Colonel Monson, that Joseph saw his opportunity. Joseph was, in Hastings's bitter words, 'the original incendiary'.[128] Hastings put Joseph's animosity down to

---

[128] Feiling, Keith (1966): *Warren Hastings*: p 139.

'my not having served him to the extent of his wishes' and to Joseph having a temper 'violent to the last degree'.

Back in England, lines had already been drawn between Hastings and his future opponents even before the Triumphirate set off. On 2 June 1773 John Walsh had criticized the small size of the council provided by the Regulating Act and the superintendence of the Governor and Council in Calcutta over Madras the other presidencies. He wrote to Joseph communicating his unease so when the new councillors arrived, Joseph was ready for them.

In April 1774, the *Anson*, carrying the judges for the Supreme Court, and the *Ashburnham* carrying the three councillors, set sail from England. Towards the end of her voyage the *Ashburnham* was nearly wrecked in a storm as she entered the River Hooghly and the councillors had to take refuge on their budgerows (capacious river boats). It was there that Joseph found them when he hurried down-river in his own budgerow to confer with them while they were stranded there and before they could reach Calcutta. By this time, Joseph, along with a seventy-year-old, very wealthy Hindu called Maharaja Nuncomar, had hatched a plan to gather witness statements in order to prove corrupt practice by Hastings, and they wanted the three councillors on their side before they started work. Joseph, Nuncomar and one Andrew Ross, a Madras merchant, were thus, again in Hastings's words, guilty of 'the first incitements' but it is unclear if Joseph was Nuncomar's tool in the subsequent conspiracy or if Nuncomar was Joseph's tool.[129] Nuncomar's association with the Company went back to the days of the Black Hole and the Battle of Plassey and he had once been a very important individual. In 1765, he had been made 'Naib Subah' or

---

[129] Feiling, Keith (1966): *Warren Hastings*: p139.

Deputy Nabob of Bengal but had lost that position and felt let down. He blamed Warren Hastings for his loss of position.[130]

Hastings's relationship with the three councillors got off to a very bad start, which was inevitable given that they were already predisposed to find fault. When they finally arrived at Calcutta, they were offended at being greeted by a seventeen-gun salute and not a twenty-one-gun salute, and there was 'no guards, no person to receive them or to show the way, no state'. Egos were bruised.

Almost the first item on the agenda when the Council met on October 24 1774, five days after the new councillors had arrived, was the Rohilla War.[131] Since the Council comprised Hastings, General Clavering, Philip Francis, Colonel Monson and Richard Barwell, an ally of Hasting, Hastings had no majority any longer, although the judges for the new Supreme Court somewhat redressed the balance of power in Hastings's favour although more broadly - the new Chief Justice, Sir Elijah Impey, was a close friend of his from Winchester School.[132] To complicate matters yet further, the judges had been granted seats on the Calcutta Council (not the Council for all India) and, to complicate matters further still, another judge was Robert Chambers, an old friend of Samuel Johnson and an acquaintance at least of Joseph Fowke.

Even if his strategic reasoning about the Rohilla War was coherent, Hastings was vulnerable over it since, by the terms of the Treaty of Benares, the Company's army had effectively been hired out to the Nawab of Oude as a mercenary force against the

---

[130] This is a simplified version of Hastings's relationship to Nuncomar and of the two men's mutual dislike. See Stephen, Sir James Fitzjames (1885): *The Story of Nuncomar and the Impeachment of Sir Elijah Impey*, pp 38-42, for a fuller account.

[131] Dalrymple, William (2019): *The Anarchy*: quoting Travers, *Ideology and Empire in Eighteenth-Century India* pp.150-1.

[132] Other fellow pupils included the historian Edward Gibbon and the poet William Cowper.

Rohillas. The Council, dominated by the Triumphirate posing as protectors of the rights of the indigenous population, replaced the Company's resident in Oudh with one of their own, John Bristow, and when the old Nawab of Oudh died in January 1775, they declared that the Treaty of Benares was a personal agreement between him and the Company and was therefore nullified by his death. They set out to negotiate a new treaty with his son and heir by which Benares would once more be removed from Oudh's authority. They also ordered that the Company army should withdraw from Rohilla land, Philip Francis describing the Rohillas as the innocent victims of unprovoked aggression when, in reality, they were the beneficiaries of a brutal Afghan incursion and ruled without the consent of the native Hindu population.

Meanwhile, Joseph and Nuncomar laboured in the background. Nuncomar used his influence to build a case against Hastings by sending threats and promises to potential witnesses. The collection of evidence became almost an industry. By early spring of 1775 a queue of sometimes as many as fifty palanquins could be seen lined up outside the door of Nuncomar's palatial house in Calcutta, each one with its potential carrier of information damaging to Hastings. The witnesses were first questioned by Nuncomar then passed on to Joseph if their evidence looked useful.

Hastings fought back tenaciously. In January, an old competitor of Nuncomar by the name of Mohan Persad, published evidence that Nuncomar had forged a bond in order to deprive the widow of a tax farmer called Bollakey Doss of a substantial part of her inheritance. If true, this was a very underhand and unpleasant act by Nuncomar because Bollakey Doss had trusted him to look after his estate. In February Mohan Persad applied to the new Supreme

Court to prosecute Nuncomar for forgery, the charge that ultimately led to his execution.[133]

Joseph, Nuncomar and the Triumphirate struck back at Hastings on 11 March 1775. That day Nuncomar offered written evidence to the Council that Hastings had taken bribes from 'Munny Begum', widow of Mir Jaffa, the former Nawab of Bengal who had been placed in office by Clive after the Battle of Plassey. Nuncomar also gave evidence that Hastings had taken bribes from Nuncomar himself, an odd but effective accusation. The Triumphirate seized on Nuncomar's evidence. They demanded that Nuncomar's accusations be heard in full Council but Hastings managed to resist, saying he refused 'to sit as chairman of what had effectively turned into a court' to try him. Hastings dissolved the Council after an all-day sitting then left, although they continued to sit unofficially without him.

It was hard to make the accusations against Hastings stick however, and it seems that Joseph's unruly temperament got the better of him. He and Nuncomar began to use undue pressure to coerce their witnesses. On 18 April, a tax farmer by the name of Kamal-ud-Din was sent by Nuncomar to Joseph's house to make a written statement that he, Kamal-ud-Din, had bribed Hastings and Hastings's fellow counsellor, Richard Barwell. However, once free of Joseph's intimidating presence, Kamal became anxious. He claimed that his statement had been made under duress and attempted to retract it, meanwhile begging Joseph for forbearance:

*I put my jamma (part of his dress) in this manner about my neck, and fell at his feet and said, "Mr. Fowke, this is all a lie. I am a poor man - don't ruin me." Mr. Fowke, hearing this, took up a book and cried*

[133] Details of the trial of Nuncomar are beyond the scope of this book. Stephen, Sir James Fitzjames (1885): *The Story of Nuncomar and the Impeachment of Sir Elijah Impey* gives a full account.

*out, "God, damn you, you son of a bitch." When he took up the book and called me names I said, "bring it, and I will seal it."*

In another account Joseph 'suddenly flew into a passion' and threw a folio volume of Churchill's *Voyages* at Kamal. It sounds in character. Also present were his son Francis, then aged twenty-two and recently arrived from England as we have seen, and Nuncomar's son-in-law, Radachurn. The incident was examined in forensic detail at the enquiry that followed.

*Quest. Who was present when the furd[134] was delivered by Mr. Fowke for you to sign?*
*Ans. It was in Mr Fowke's house, a number of people were going backwards and forwards.*
*Quest. In what room was the furd delivered?*
*Ans. In the bedchamber.*
*Quest. Was Mr. Fowke present when you signed your name to the arzee?*
*Ans. I signed it in the veranda. Mr Fowke was in his own room. Both the arzees were sealed in presence of Mr. Francis Fowke and not of Mr. Joseph Fowke.*
*Quest. In what room was the seal put to these papers?*
*Ans. In Mr. Francis Fowke's room about ten or eleven when Camaul O Deen had come to the house.*
*Quest. Are you sure it was not on the veranda?*
*Ans. No, it was not on the veranda.*
*Quest. Does Mr. Francis Fowke's room open on the veranda?*
*Ans. No, you go through the hall to Mr. Francis Fowke's room...[135]*

According to Kamal, he signed the false statement so as to escape Joseph's pressure, but then asked Francis Fowke to return it to him. Francis, who comes across as something of a peacemaker,

---

[134] An affidavit or statement. 'Arzee' had a similar meaning.

[135] Anonymous (1786): *The Trial of Joseph Fowke, etc:* pp 6-8.

persuaded him to return for it the next day, 19 October, but when Kamal returned with some of his men to try to retrieve the document he found the Fowkes, Nuncomar and Rada Churn 'in consultation' in Joseph's house and they refused to hand it over. There followed a scuffle between Kamal's men and those of Joseph, and Kamal was forced to beat a retreat in his palanquin. He went directly to the Council to demand justice, his face pale and his clothes torn. The next day, witnesses were interrogated at the house of Judge Elijah Impey by Impey and his fellow judges of the Supreme Court in their dual capacity as Justices of the Peace for Calcutta. The investigation started at ten in the morning and continued until eleven at night and when it was over, Hastings and his colleague Barwell were given four days in which to decide whether to proceed to a prosecution against their accusers. The accused were granted bail. On 23 April, Hastings and Barwell decided in favour of the prosecution of Nuncomar, Radachurn and Joseph Fowke but the charges against Francis Fowke were dropped.

Events accelerated. On 6 May, Nuncomar was arrested for forgery committed in order to deprive the widow of Bollakey Doss of her inheritance, a capital offence. He was imprisoned in the common jail. His trial started on June 6th, continuing over Sunday 11th, and finished on June 16th, when he was found guilty. It was held in the Assembly Rooms, usually the site for balls and other social gatherings, and was the one of the first and most celebrated sittings of the new High Court. The transposition of European legal practice to an Indian setting was far from easy. The judges 'wore their heavy wigs and (tradition says) retired three or four times daily to change their linen ... the jury from time to time retired to an adjoining room to take refreshment or sleep'.136 Hastings's testimony at the trial touched on Joseph Fowke:

*Q. Did you ever know him guilty of any dishonest or dishonourable act?*
*A. It is a difficult question. I will not pretend to say I know him guilty of either ... I have always considered him of a violent and morose temper; and, while under the influence, too apt to insinuate actions in which he is concerned to base and bad motives in others. I do not recollect any dishonest or dishonourable acts, but he is violent to the last degree.*

Following the guilty verdict, on 22nd June, Nuncomar's attorney, Thomas Farrer, appealed for an 'arrest of judgement' but Farrer had little hope of success. In a note to himself, written that day, there was little expectation of leniency:

*'Sentence per chief justice – a definitive sentence. Must not expect mercy - death'.*

On 24 June, leave for appeal was rejected and then, on 6 July, the trial of Joseph Fowke, Nuncomar and Radachurun for conspiracy against Warren Hastings began, Nuncomar, under threat of imminent execution, being taken from prison for the occasion. The trial was held under the three High Court judges. All three accused – Joseph, Nuncomar and Radachurn – were found innocent of conspiracy against Warren Hastings on July 10th . Their trial for conspiracy against Richard Barlow 'began and ended' three days later and this time all three were found guilty. Joseph's punishment was a fine of fifty rupees. The reason for this leniency was not his acquaintance with Judge Robert Chambers; it was because his nephew, William Holland (his sister Sophia's son), then the Company Resident at Dacca, threatened Richard Barlow with

---

136 Stephen, Sir James Fitzjames (1885): *The Story of Nuncomar and the Impeachment of Sir Elijah Impey*: p 104.

exposure of Barlow's own corruption in Dacca if Barlow chose to demand a more punitive fine.

Meanwhile Nuncomar languished in jail. On August 1, his petition against the death penalty was rejected and on August 5 1775 at around 8.30am, he was taken to the 'place of execution' in his palanquin to the 'howlings and lamentations of the poor wretched people who were taking their last leave of him', thence onto the gallows 'looking around him with perfect unconcern'. He met his death with great dignity: 'his composure was wonderful; not a sigh escaped him, nor the slightest alteration of voice or countenance'.[137] A servant put a kerchief over his face, he gave the signal and was hanged.[138]

Nuncomar's execution was a stain on Hastings's character and was used against him repeatedly over the coming years. That Nuncomar was guilty of the forgery was well established but he had been accused under an English law that should not have had authority in India, as Judge Robert Chambers pointed out in a minority opinion. By this debateable means, it was argued by his enemies, Hastings rid himself of a key hostile witness in the proceedings against him for bribery brought by his fellow councillors. To balance this, Hastings's friends pointed out that he had not been a judge at the trial and had kept at a proper distance from the proceedings and so could not be accused of influencing them. The bitterness festered. In April 1776, Joseph wrote to Samuel Johnson enclosing a bundle of documents and asking Johnson to prepare a sympathetic account for publication. Johnson declined, explaining that he was also a friend of Warren Hastings and he could not take sides:

---

[137] Stephen, Sir James Fitzjames (1885): *The Story of Nuncomar and the Impeachment of Sir Elijah Impey*: p 239.

[138] Stephen, Sir James Fitzjames (1885): *The Story of Nuncomar and the Impeachment of Sir Elijah Impey*: p 240.

*To your former letter I made no answer, because I had none to make. Of the death of the unfortunate man [Nuncomar] I believe Europe thinks as you think; but it was past prevention; and it was not fit for me to move a question in public which I was not qualified to discuss ... Let me know, dear Sir, what you are doing. Are you accumulating gold, or picking up diamonds? Or are you now sated with Indian wealth, and content with what you have? Have you vigour for bustle, or tranquillity for inaction? Whatever you do, I do not suspect you of pillaging or oppressing; and shall rejoice to see you return with a body unbroken, and a mind uncorrupted.*[139]

That August 1775, the day following Nuncomar's execution, Francis Fowke was appointed to be the Company's Resident at Benares to implement the provisions of the Treaty of Fyzabad, which had been negotiated by the Council dominated by the Triumphirate against Hastings's opposition and which undid much of the substance of the Treaty of Benares. He was appointed due to the influence of Joseph's friend General Clavering, the senior member of the Triumphirate, and Joseph joined him in Benares shortly after, hoping to continue his trade in diamonds - but all the while nurturing greater ambitions. It was during this year that John Walsh proposed Joseph for Governor of Madras.[140]

Writing to Francis from his London house in Chesterfield Street, John Walsh emphasised the connection with the Triumphirate:

*General Clavering and Mr Francis ... are particular friends of ours and will be ready to render you any service in their power*[141]

Meanwhile Margaret Fowke, aged eighteen, had embarked at Gravesend with the help and support of Walsh and in hopes of

---

139 *Gentleman's Magazine* Vol 87, part 2, p. 528-9.

140 Mss Eur Kaye, Minor Collections, Handlists: abstract of the Fowke Mss. p 65.

141 Mss Eur Kaye, Minor Collections, Mss 20-44, 72: 20 March 1774.

being reunited with Francis. Kitty Treacher's death had made it easier for her to be with her father should that prove necessary since there would now be no young stepmother of questionable breeding to defer to.

# 9. Margaret and Francis in India

Francis, Arthur and Margaret Fowke, Joseph's three children by Elizabeth Walsh/Fowke, went out to India within a few years of each other, as we have seen: in 1773, 1774/5 and 1776 respectively. Francis and Arthur and their father may have been reunited briefly in Calcutta on Arthur's arrival when Arthur was already terribly ill but, as we know, Arthur died shortly after. It was in late 1775, while Francis established himself in Benares following Nuncomar's execution, that Margaret planned her departure. Her intention was to stay initially with her aunt Mrs Sophia Holland, her father Joseph's sister, in Madras.

Margaret had survived her rather odd childhood in the great houses of John Walsh, and, to a lesser extent, Margaret Clive and Jenny Lathom/Lady Strachey. The incident with the imaginary highwayman and the fire in Reading notwithstanding, she had grown up to be a young woman of character. She was tall and fair like her mother Liz Walsh/Fowke, loved riding, spoke and wrote fluent French and played the piano beautifully. By December 1775 her passage was booked on the *Camden* and she was to be accompanied by Miss Pybus, daughter of a friend of the Clives.[142] Mindful, as were all the Fowkes, of the value of their connection with Lady Clive, Margaret stayed with her at Oakley Park in

---

142 EUR, Kaye: Minor Collections: p75.

Shropshire for seven weeks before she sailed. Oakley Park was where Margaret Clive had retreated after Robert Clive's death almost exactly a year earlier.

Unfortunately, on landing at Madras, Margaret discovered that Sophia Holland had died so she sailed on to join her father in Calcutta. Events, as was so common at that time, moved faster than the power of the protagonists to communicate with each other and when she arrived in Calcutta she discovered that both her father and brother had moved to Benares, as we have seen. She stayed temporarily with a family friend, Mrs Lacam. It was not an easy time for her; her first days in India were marred by Warren Hastings's understandable hostility as she described in a letter to Walsh:

> *It is a custom when any ladies arrive in Calcutta for the Governor either to pay a formal visit or leave his card for them & afterwards invite them to his balls and concerts – Mr Hastings omitted his ceremony to me & when I have met him in publick he has gone and made his bow to every lady as they sat & passed me … because of his publick dispute with my father.* [143]

Everything changed towards the end of 1776 when Colonel Monson, the third of the Triumphirate, died and Warren Hastings once more had a majority on the Council. That December he used his casting vote to replace Francis Fowke in Benares with his own man, as Joseph reported to John Walsh in January 1777, Francis having already left to return to Calcutta:

> *Sir, I lose no time in acquainting you with the steps taken to ruin me and my family … They appointed Mr Thomas Graham Resident in his [Francis Fowke's] room with young Barwell for his assistant. They could*

---

[143] Eur D456: Correspondence of the Fowke, Benn, Walsh and Maskelyne familes, Vol. 10, p 4: Margaret Fowke to John Walsh, near Calcutta, 18 December 1776.

*find no fault in his [Francis's] conduct, and therefore you may be assured*
*their whole view was to distress me and have creatures of their own in*
*this part of the world to answer their own particular purposes ... should*
*the Rajah refuse to comply, a thing not very likely, I suppose I shall be*
*ordered away as my son has been. I was put into the house I inhabit by*
*the Rajah at the request of Mr Hastings at a time he thought I was*
*supported in Europe. I have been prevented by a wicked influence in*
*purchasing more than 16,000 rupees worth of diamonds in ten months*
*... I have done my duty as a citizen & hereafter let murders, rapines*
*& theft spread all over India I shall look on with stoical indifference.*
*But this I will venture to pronounce on taking leave, that if the East*
*Indiamen in England continue to support the most execrable traitors to*
*their country in opposition to one of the noblest ... for my own part I*
*would as soon embrace a pickpocket as the man who will declare himself*
*an enemy to General Clavering or strike at the fame of the illustrious*
*Monson ... all my friends together will scarcely save me against the*
*inveterate malice of Hastings & Barwell. The former pursues me like a*
*fury ...*
*I am sincerely, Dear Sir, your faithful humble servant, Joseph Fowke*[144]

Brother and sister were reunited under one roof in Calcutta and
Joseph joined them from Benares shortly after. All three shared a
passion for music, both men playing violin and cello and Margaret
playing the harpsichord and, soon, the piano - and both men had
some skill at the keyboard also. Francis was in many ways the
perfect elder brother. He was kind and caring, very clever, had a
mild disposition and was 'much given to flattery and railing'.
Throughout Margaret's life he was her closest friend and her
mentor, advising her on music and other matters even if they
disagreed on religion. (He was a sceptic and she was a believer.) At

---

[144] Eur D456: Correspondence of the Fowke, Benn, Walsh and Maskelyne
familes, Vol. 10, p 8: Joseph Fowke to John Walsh, Benares 11 January 1777
(received 2 October 1777).

one point in later life she even tried to persuade him to move in with her and her husband in London or, to be more precise, she tried to persuade him to take rooms round the corner but to spend his daylight hours with them, with a room in her house set aside for his use which was particularly suitable for music.

Life in Calcutta in the 1770s was very sociable. We should imagine Joseph, Francis and Margaret at frequent musical soirées and balls, Francis and Joseph smoking hookahs, a habit almost universal among European men in India at that time. A note from Francis to Margaret gives a flavour of the time:

*If the review be upon the esplanade … I can carry you in my palanquin to Mr Auriol's ball.*

There were intrigues – Margaret had two offers of marriage – and scandals: her friend Charlotte Webb disgraced herself in some way with her brother-in-law and was sent off to Madras, a nasty tangle to get into in any century. A note from her to Margaret sheds a little light:

*I have a great favour to request, to despatch a billet doux to Mr Evans [Miss Webb's brother-in-law] Wonder not at me nor at my extravagant action ... I after this billet have done with this gentleman.*[145]

At some point in the later part of the 1770s, the three of them moved upriver to the Dutch settlement at Chinsura, perhaps because it was cheaper to live there. There they became friendly with a Mrs Van Dankleman who lived very elegantly but alone. Her husband had been chief of the settlement before being summoned to Dutch Batavia (Jakarta) to answer 'some accusations against him' and had not been 'heard of thereafter'. Meanwhile John Walsh was active in London on Francis's behalf, lobbying the Directors and

---

[145] EUR, Kaye, Minor Collections, Fowke Mss p 185: Charlotte Webb to Miss Fowke.

members of Parliament and ministers. The struggle with Hastings continued and no one had complete ascendancy. In 1777 Hastings was censured by the Directors and ordered to reinstate Francis at Benares but Hastings ignored the order, estimating that his standing with the Indian rulers would be damaged if he gave way and, on balance, losing standing in India was the greater evil. The councillors in Calcutta reinforced the Directors' order with a motion in council for Francis's restoration, proposed by Philip Francis on 5th April 1779, but this also failed.

Meanwhile the Company's forces had become engaged in open warfare with the Marathas, who threatened British interests in Benares and Oudh and as far east as Bombay. (From a Maratha perspective of course, the Company was the threatening presence.) Bombay was particularly vulnerable and, following a treaty between the French and the Maratha government of Poona in 1776, a Company army based in Bombay attacked pre-emptively. It advanced slowly into Maratha territory but was forced to retreat and sue for terms. The Treaty of Wadgaon which followed was signed locally on 16 January 1779 but Hastings back in Calcutta rejected it. On Hastings's orders, Colonel Thomas Goddard counter-attacked with a force of six thousand troops and captured Ahmedabad, to the north of Bombay. That was on February 15, 1779; by 11 December of the following year Goddard had captured Bassein, now part of the suburbs of Bombay, stopping the immediate Maratha threat.

However, the Marathas were far from being a spent force and successful prosecution of the war had become Hastings's urgent priority. He needed a clear mandate and could not risk being undermined by his remaining enemy on the Council, Joseph Fowke's ally Philip Francis. On Christmas Day 1780, Hastings's and Francis's agents met and agreed a truce between them, a truce that was sealed by dinner between the two principles the following day, Boxing Day. Under the terms of this Christmas truce, Philip

Francis agreed to support all Hastings's measures for prosecution of the war with the Marathas and Hastings agreed to the return of Francis Fowke to Benares. He also offered a salaried job to Joseph. The job involved cataloguing minutes of the Directors' proceedings and Joseph reluctantly accepted the 'paltry salary' although it was really quite magnanimous considering Joseph's hostility.[146] By that time, Joseph was isolated. General Clavering and Colonel Monson were both dead and he had fallen out with Philip Francis, now the only remaining member of the Triumphirate and the only leading figure opposed to Hastings. Philip Francis had 'betrayed me and left me a wreck'; he was 'as little cut out for action as a monkey'.[147]

Francis Fowke enjoyed under a year of his second residence at Benares. In May 1780, Philip Francis reneged on the Christmas agreement with Hastings and refused to back further expenditure for the war against the Marathas. In due course, Francis Fowke found himself recalled once more. The problems of the war were so pressing that Hastings, having suffered years of vicious opposition, could take no more. He decided that the only way out of the conflict between him and Philip Francis was that one or the other should die. He insulted Francis in a memorandum to the Council; Francis had been 'void of truth and honour'. Francis took the bait and responded by challenging Hastings to a duel.

At 5.30 am on 16th August the two principal members of the Calcutta Council met in the grey light of morning on the Alipur Road, two middle-aged men, neither of them with much interest in exercise or fighting. Francis had never fired a pistol before and Hastings could remember doing so only once or twice. Their seconds measured fourteen paces then they took their places.

---

[146] Feiling, Keith (1966): *Warren Hastings*: pp 220-21.

[147] Eur D456: Correspondence of the Fowke, Benn, Walsh and Maskelyne familes: Vol. 12, p 12: Joseph Fowke to John Walsh, 10 October 1780.

Hastings deferred his fire while Francis misfired twice. The third time they both fired almost simultaneously. Francis narrowly missed but Hastings's bullet struck Francis on the right side and lodged under his left shoulder blade.

'I'm dead,' Francis cried and fell to the ground.

'Good God, I hope not!' called Hastings and hurried over. Having checked on the damage, he rushed home in his palanquin and sent for the surgeon general and his own doctor to attend the victim. Philip Francis staged a remarkably swift recovery but he left for England in December and from that point on, Hastings finally had full control of the Council, really for the first time since he had been appointed Governor General. In January 1781, Francis Fowke was recalled from Benares. It was for reasons of state and not because of personal animosity between him and Hastings, as Francis made clear in a letter to John Walsh:

> *I cannot but observe with gratitude the great moderation he has shown in a victory so complete ... over the party we had so warmly espoused ... I believe he has no personal dislike of me ... I doubt however if the impression of injuries offered him by my father is entirely effaced from his heart ... my father has been so very intimate, and successively had such violent quarrels with a great number of people...[148]*

Joseph was less forgiving. Back in Calcutta, when not cataloguing the Directors' proceedings, he continued a correspondence with Chait Singh, the Rajah of Benares, in which he implied that Hastings was about to be recalled by the Directors in London and so could be safely ignored. Meanwhile, things were almost back to normal. Brother, sister and father re-established themselves in Calcutta and Joseph took on the former house of the Scottish artist

---

[148] Eur D456: Correspondence of the Fowke, Benn, Walsh and Maskelyne familes, Vol. 13 (continued), p. 149: Francis Fowke to John Walsh, Calcutta, 30 May 1781.

John Thomas Seaton. Joseph continued to write letters bemoaning his situation but things could have been worse, as Margaret described to John Walsh:

> *...besides the happiness of my brother's company, I derive this further advantage from his removal to Calcutta, that the circle of my acquaintance is much enlarged ... our house is in that part of town which commands a fine view of the beautiful river ... I ride pretty much frequently in the season of the year which will admit of it ... I have written to Lady Clive by this conveyance.*[149]

Lady Clive sent Margaret a necklace containing diamonds that had once belonged to Margaret's mother, described in a letter from Lady Clive to John Walsh:

> *Dear Cousin,*
> *Not knowing what to send my dear Miss Fowke as a token of remembrance & affection, I bethought myself I had some pretty trifling diamond which formerly came from our aunt Maskelyne and as this way of disposing of them must be agreeable to those so beloved shades, could they be consulted, I have, with a small addition of diamonds, made a very pretty jeweller ornament to hang to Miss Fowke's neck. I desire you to take the greatest care that it be safely conveyed to that young lady.*[150]

There were further gifts from Lady Clive, including a portrait of Lord Clive for Francis, which was captured by Spanish pirates while being transported to India, until eventually ransomed 'in a

---

[149] Eur D456: Correspondence of the Fowke, Benn, Walsh and Maskelyne familes: Vol. 11, p 46: Margaret Fowke to John Walsh, Calcutta 19 February 1782.

[150] Eur D456: Correspondence of the Fowke, Benn, Walsh and Maskelyne familes: Vol. 9, p 89: Lady Clive to John Walsh, Claremont, 26 May 1780.

perfect state of preservation' by Walsh for sixteen guineas and sent on its way, reaching its new owner in 1782.[151]

Francis had sired an illegitimate son, William, while at Benares whom he sent back to England in 1783 probably aged twelve with his cousin William Holland who sailed for home at that time.[152] Back in Mayfair, where William Holland settled with his own two white and three illegitimate mixed-race children, little William Fowke was soon absorbed into the noisy, exuberant household, with trips to the seaside, quarrels and laughter. William Fowke's colouring is unknown but it is likely that he was half-Indian.

Fowke allies in England, Walsh in particular, were still working on their behalf and in 1783 Hastings no longer felt able to obstruct an order from the Directors to reappoint Francis to Benares for a third time. Possibly also, any lingering animosity on his part towards the Fowkes had been dissipated by Francis and Margaret's pleasant manners. Francis left on 11th April. Margaret was devastated, writing to him the day after his departure

*'I will resist my grief ... You may suppose I passed a restless night after you left me ... Who would not feel the same, when they lose a constant companion whom they most tenderly love...*[153]

She lost no time in making plans to follow and by 2nd September 1783 she had set off for what would prove to be the journey of a lifetime. She sailed up the Ganges in the party of Judge Robert Chambers and his young wife, Sophia. Chambers had been one of the judges at Joseph's trial for conspiracy but, as we have seen,

---

[151] Eur D456: Correspondence of the Fowke, Benn, Walsh and Maskelyne familes: Vol. 13 Francis Fowke to John Walsh, Calcutta, 30 May 1781.

[152] A will of Francis, dated 1781, left his estate to be divided equally between his sister Margaret and little William.

[153] EUR, Kaye: Minor Collections, Fowke Mss, p 116: Margaret Fowke to Francis Fowke, Calcutta, 12 April 1783.

both Chambers and Joseph were friends of Samuel Johnson and they saw each other frequently in Calcutta. Margaret's departure had not been easy and Joseph had resisted vehemently. She was a comfort to him and a companion and he was very proud of her interest in music - and she perhaps helped to keep his gambling under control. Her letters to Francis form a running commentary:

*Last night at the Williams we met Mrs Tolly who played and sang on her guitar. After Miss Webb's divine performance no one gives much satisfaction ... I begin to have innumerable difficulties with my father ... tells me there is great impropriety in my going out without him ... that my uncle ought to be hanged for not educating me more piously ... yet I shall persist in endeavouring to obtain my liberty...[154]*

*He spoke against the impropriety of my going up in such company .. and said General C [Clavering] wd rather have seen his daughters in flames than in such a situation ... He flew into the most violent rage imaginable, said ... that I might go butt that he never wished to see my face again, that I should be his death.[155]*

*We had a little party here last night – the Days, Hays and Williams. I had the violins & Diehle ... Birch was here last night. He is a card player, which is a very good introduction. My father plays exceedingly high. His card purse is at present very low...[156]*

*The card party was here. I make a point of behaving very politely & good-naturedly to them – yet I do not like their society.[157]*

[154] EUR, Kaye: Minor Collections, Fowke Mss, p 116: Margaret Fowke to Francis Fowke, Calcutta, April 1783.

[155] EUR, Kaye: Minor Collections, Fowke Mss, p 121: Margaret Fowke to Francis Fowke Calcutta, April 1783 '

[156] EUR, Kaye: Minor Collections, Fowke Mss, p 117-8: Margaret Fowke to Francis Fowke, Calcutta, 3 May 1783.

[157] EUR, Kaye: Minor Collections, Fowke Mss, p 117-8: Margaret Fowke to Francis Fowke, Calcutta, 18 May 1783.

*My father continues card playing. He plays very high & did bet high, but he has now declared he will never bet again. His winnings amount to ten thousand rupees and he says he will never risk any money but this little bank. I fancy this would prove a loser's vow were he to have a run against him.[158]*

Then, when she thought he would never give way and she would have to attend card parties forever, he suddenly buckled:

*I never saw such an astonishing change. He then very calmly spoke of my journey, of the little real danger...[159]*

One hurdle was crossed but poor Margaret now had other difficulties. Robert Chambers expected Margaret to be company for his beautiful wife Sophia, but Sophia was perhaps a little too beautiful for her own good. Margaret used her skill at the keyboard to attract the young men; Sophia had no need for such devices. Although married, a mysterious 'Mrs D' seems to have almost led her astray:

*Poor Sir Robert is dangerously ill ... Lady Chambers has lost her reputation entirely. I hope she has not lost her honour ... In an evil hour Sir Robert asked Mrs D into his family. In fact it was asking a woman of art & gallantry to be the friend & directress of a young and handsome wife.[160]*

Sophia's problems dissipated and Sir Robert got better. They set out. The journey up the Ganges was delightful. They travelled in a flotilla of budgerows with many servants and all conveniences.

---

[158] EUR, Kaye: Minor Collections, Fowke Mss, p 119: Margaret to Francis Fowke Calcutta, 11 July 1783.

[159] EUR, Kaye: Minor Collections, Fowke Mss, p 122: Margaret Fowke to Francis Fowke, Calcutta, 1 September 1783.

[160] EUR, Kaye: Minor Collections, Fowke Mss, p 119: Margaret either to John Walsh or to Francis Fowke, July 1783.

Joseph had arranged for some of Margaret's baggage to follow her but she brought her musical instruments and at least one musician on the river with her, writing ahead to Francis from Boglepur:

*My father writes me word that your 2 boxes ... a violincello & a fiddler at 100 rupees a month were to leave Calcutta on the 4th. I shall certainly not keep the harper – he has been very useful on this journey...*[161]

Sophia Chambers or 'Fanny' was near to Margaret in age, and one of the most beautiful women in Calcutta (Joseph flirted with her at any opportunity and called her his 'sultana') but her husband Robert and Margaret were more suited intellectually. When the expedition made camp on the banks of the river each afternoon, the two of them would search out historic sites and monuments leaving Sophia behind.

All things Indian were of interest to educated members of the European community at that time and ethnographic enquiries had become fashionable. The Asiatic Society, founded the following year, was at the heart of such research and constituted the first systematic attempt by Europeans to understand Asian culture. The founder was Sir William Jones, a puisne (subordinate) judge at the Supreme Court that year who brought with him a scholarly interest in Asian cultures. An impressive intellectual, his mother tongues were Welsh and English but eventually he was expert in eight languages including Persian, Latin, Greek, Arabic and Hebrew and had a working knowledge of a further twelve. The founding meeting of the Society was held on 15th January 1784 in the Grand Jury Room of the Supreme Court. Thirty Calcutta residents

---

[161] EUR, Kaye: Minor Collections, Fowke Mss, p 124: Margaret Fowke to Francis Fowke, near Boglepore, 12 October 1783.

gathered under the chairmanship of Sir Robert Chambers, by then returned from his trip to Benares with Margaret.[162]

When the Chamberses and Margaret reached Benares, they found that Francis had set himself up in the house of the former resident, Hastings's protégée Mr Markham, son of the Archbishop of York. They all lodged with him there and Robert Chambers spent much of his time acquiring Sanskrit manuscripts. To suit Margaret, once the Chamberses were gone Francis moved to a more agreeable location outside the town. Brother and sister would ride together in the cool of the early mornings and quickly resumed their close relationship, probably grateful for their father's absence although he must have played a large part in their conversation. She was twenty-six and had already spent eight years in India and he was thirty-one.

Music was their common passion. Among Margaret's favourite composers were Purcell, Handel, Haydn, Pleyel and Correlli. Meanwhile Francis was working on his paper *On the Vina or Indian Lyre*, the first serious attempt by a European to comprehend and quantify the differences between European and Indian musical traditions and to describe aspects of Indian music in European terms. It was published in the first issue of the Journal of the Asiatic Society in 1788, courtesy of Sir William Jones.

Margaret collected Indian music. She organised musicians to play for her so that she could take down what they were playing and she sometimes played along with them. From these tunes, converted to European musical notation, she produced a collection of 'Hindoostani Airs'. These were very much in the European tradition despite the name but they impressed Sir

---

[162] The Asiatic Society continued to meet at the Court building until 1796 when it built its own premises. Its aims were wide: 'The bounds of investigations will be the geographical limits of Asia, and within these limits its enquiries will be extended to whatever is performed by man or produced by nature' (*Memorandum of Articles* of the Asiatic Society).

William Jones, and Joseph Fowke sent a bound copy to Lady Clive in England. Margaret was not alone in this occupation. Famously, Sophia Plowden, whom Margaret knew well and who corresponded with her about music, collected and annotated the music of nautch girls and performers at the court of Oudh in Lucknow around this time, in particular the songs of the famous courtesan, Khanum Jan.[163]

In November 1784 Warren Hastings arrived in Benares for a two-month visit in order to conduct negotiations with the Nawab of Oudh. This was in the last year of Hastings's period of office in India when his wife Marian, the former Baroness Imhoff, had already left for home. Hastings made his way up river, disembarking at Benares on 17th February. At his first stop on the journey he had received a letter from Edward Wheler, a member of the Council, asking him to allow Joseph Fowke to visit his children at Benares - which Hastings refused because Joseph had maintained that subversive correspondence with Rajah Chait Singh, whom Hastings had deposed as ruler of Benares in 1781. Hastings's refusal of Joseph's request does not seem to have marred his relationship with Joseph's children and he must have approved of their rather scholarly and genteel way of life at Benares. The understanding was mutual: Margaret sent him her Hindoostani airs and advice on music and Francis ordered a print of a portrait of Hastings by the painter Zoffany.

The reasons for Rajah Chait Singh's removal from power during Hastings's visit of 1781, were muddled. More accurately, Chait Singh had fled house arrest (something of a paradox for a sovereign prince) following a chaotic but bloody episode involving the death of around two hundred British sepoys. A Nawab

---

163https://blogs.bl.uk/asian-and-african/2018/06/sophia-plowden-khanum-jan-and-hindustani-airs.html - blog by musician and writer, Katherine Butler Schofield.

(deputy) had been appointed in his place but had proved to be incompetent and corrupt, and a period of misrule had followed. The Nawab had been replaced by a new Nawab by the name of Ali Ibrahim Khan and under Ibrahim Kahn's rule, Benares began to prosper again. However the countryside around it was devasted by famine and misrule, the country people fleeing at the sight of soldiers, many of whom were unpaid. Through all this turbulence, Francis Fowke, as the Company's Resident at Benares, pursued a moderate course which may also have led Hastings to feel sympathetically towards him. Hastings praised Francis for his 'gentleness of manners'.

Alone back in Calcutta, Joseph pursued his usual interests, in particular music and cards. Margaret had learned to be sceptical:

> … *notwithstanding this, I am apt to imagine he follows these calm pleasures only from necessity. He is naturally restless & likes to be engaged in scenes of great bustle.*[164]

Joseph particularly revered Handel, whom he remembered seeing as a youth, and he disdained the new 'gallant' style of music of Haydn and others, then just coming into fashion. This was a common prejudice among the older generation of music lovers, who felt that the younger set lacked gravitas and that audiences at concerts of the new music failed to listen with proper concentration. Joseph and his friends associated the new style with the young women who played the harpsichords and pianos and who, between pieces, gossiped about the latest fashions - in clothing as well as music – young women such as Margaret.

Even before Margaret left for Benares, Joseph was gambling high. Once she was gone, he sought to reassure her that he had it

---

[164] Eur D456: Correspondence of the Fowke, Benn, Walsh and Maskelyne familes: Vol. 11, p 88: Margaret Fowke to John Walsh, Calcutta, 6 February 1783.

under control. Mrs van Dankleman, their Dutch friend, widow of a former Governor of Chinsura, also tried to reassure her, writing from Calcutta:

*We make it a point amusing him in hopes to keep him from gaming. I flatter myself we have succeeded a little … Your father and I have again practised Chess this morning for more than four hours … Lady Chambers says it is good for us both, she was busy in the cellar and sent him to me.*[165]

But in the summer of 1785, it all went horribly wrong. For the second time in his life, Joseph lost a very large sum of money, 'a lach & 40,000 rupees'. Francis's cousin and friend, William Holland, wrote from London when he heard the news:

*What a madman, I hope however that you will not enable him to pay his losses either from your own money or from mine.*[166]

Joseph fell ill, perhaps as a result of the strain; Francis ignored William's advice and kept his father afloat. There followed several months' uncertainty but by December 1785 Joseph had recovered 'from the jaws of death'.[167]

Meanwhile, in August 1785 after Margaret had been in Benares for nearly two years and immediately following the news of Joseph's latest disastrous losses at the card table, Francis and Margaret made plans for home. They returned to Calcutta that autumn while Joseph still lay on his sick bed and in December, shortly after his recovery, they sailed on the *Dublin*, having booked the 'roundhouse', the most prestigious cabin on the ship.

---

[165] EUR, Kaye: Minor Collections, Fowke Mss, p 139: Mrs von Dankleman to Margaret Fowke, Calcutta, Monday 29(?) 1784.

[166] EUR, Kaye: Minor Collections, Fowke Mss, DII: 7 August 1785, William Holland to Francis Fowke.

[167] EUR, Kaye: Minor Collections, Fowke Mss: p 153: Captain John Garston to Francis Fowke, 30 December 1785, Patna.

Accompanying them was Francis's 'adjutant' or secretary, previously the secretary of John Markham, a young man by the name of John Benn originally from Ormathwaite in the Lake District. Benn's father had died just before he was born and he had been brought up by his uncle, Dr William Brownrigg, the chemist, famous among other achievements as being the first person to identify platinum as an element. Through Dr Brownrigg's friend John Robinson MP, Lord North's private secretary, Benn had obtained a post with the Company and had arrived in Calcutta in 1778.

Benn had made almost as much money in India as had Francis, who left with between £50,000 and £70,000.[168] In 1773 Warren Hastings had taken over production of opium for the East India Company. Trade with China had become one of the Company's most significant activities, in particular the acquisition of tea for sale in Britain and elsewhere, and opium from India was much in demand in China, so this was a way to boost the Company's revenue, or rather, to avoid depleting it. Production was mainly at Patna, downstream from Benares. At Patna, the opium juice was dried in the sun then moulded into cakes. Hastings sold the monopoly first to a Mr Mackenzie, who later sold it on to Hastings's servant Sulivan who quickly made a large sum and sold it on to John Benn. Benn sold it on almost immediately for another large profit.

Love was in the air, or the eighteenth-century version of that virtue. Francis described Benn in a letter to John Walsh:

> … *a young man of a very large fortune. He has a very good classical education, his morals are unexceptional … his temper is remarkably*

---

[168] The number differs between sources.

*even and good ... yet I must confess, his mind and manners are defective
in that refinement and engaging polish ...'[169]*

In other words he was not quite a good enough match for Francis's
sister as far as Francis was concerned, but he would do. John Benn
was perhaps a little dull beside the gifted brother and sister but he
turned out to be very good for Margaret and was perhaps the best
she could get. Anyway, he fully supported her in her musical
ambitions and cared for her during the pains of multiple still births
to come.

Joseph was devastated when Francis and Margaret sailed. He
was a difficult father but that did not mean that he lacked love for
his children. He wrote to Walsh in a letter that Margaret took with
her on the ship:

*This comes by the hand of my daughter who is accompanied by her
brother. Such a separation at my time of life is piercing; but it is an evil
which necessity compels me to yield to. The miserable prospect this country
affords gives no encouragement for a wise man to stay in it ... I hope by
my stay here still to be able to add something to her comforts, for a soul
great and generous like her own must and ought to be supplied with the
means of preserving an independency. She is indeed the very exact copy
of her mother.[170]*

Two years later, in 1788, Joseph too set sail, ending his third and
last stay in India. He had been born there in 1716, had left in 1728
aged twelve, had returned in 1736, then had left again with
Elizabeth Walsh/Fowke in 1751. In 1771 he had returned again to

---

[169] Eur D456: Correspondence of the Fowke, Benn, Walsh and Maskelyne
familes: Vol. 12, p 202: Francis Fowke to John Walsh 10 August 1786, written
aboard the *Dublin*.

[170] Eur D456: Correspondence of the Fowke, Benn, Walsh and Maskelyne
familes: Vol. 12 (cont), p 136: Joseph Fowke to John Walsh, Calcutta, 3
October 1786.

repair his fortune and now it was over, a total of forty-four years, more than half his life, and he was worth a mere £1,400. Some of his musical instruments were advertised for sale in the Calcutta press, auctioneer Burrell and Gould, and the advertisement perhaps provides a better epitaph for Joseph's stay in India than do his quarrels:

*A remarkable toned harpsichord, maker Kirkman, a very fine violincello, & one a Stradivaries, Handel's songs in 5 vols with all the accompaniments in 6 parts.*

The journey was unpleasant and he fell out with the captain, writing ahead to Francis from St. Helena:

*I write this to inform you that I arrived yesterday at this place in health after a 16 weeks passage wanting 2 days from Bombay. Words cannot convey an idea of the brutality of Captain Horncastle to me and all his passengers ... I wonder that I have escaped madness after all the crosses and mortifications I have met with.[171]*

He landed at Dartmouth on 20 August 1788 'in a Deal cutter ... most heartily rejoiced at being released from the society of a sea monster'.[172] Margaret, writing to Francis, then in Brighton, before Joseph had landed, had the last word:

*Perhaps before this reaches you, the man of many conflicts will be arrived.[173]*

---

[171] Eur D456: Correspondence of the Fowke, Benn, Walsh and Maskelyne families: Vol. 31, p 71: Joseph Fowke to Francis his son St Helena, 13 June 1788:

[172] Eur D456: Correspondence of the Fowke, Benn, Walsh and Maskelyne families: Vol. 31, p 83: Joseph Fowke to Francis Fowke, Dartmouth, 20 August 1788.

[173] Eur D456: Correspondence of the Fowke, Benn, Walsh and Maskelyne families: Vol. 31, p 73: Margaret Fowke to Francis Fowke 20 August 1788.

# 10. Back in England

Francis Fowke, Margaret Fowke and John Benn disembarked in England on 29th September 1786, and on 30th June of the following year, Margaret and John Benn were married. The ceremony was marred by the absence of John Walsh. Walsh felt slighted. He was very aware that, without his protective influence, his nephew and niece would not have flourished as they had done, returning in state in the roundhouse of the ship, Francis having accumulated enough money that he need never work again. It was the Clive influence but John Walsh in particular, which had made it all possible. He complained that Margaret had not written frequently enough (she claimed that her letters had gone missing) and, now that brother and sister were back in England, he said they hardly bothered to visit him. They had come to Warfield Park shortly after they landed but, after that, only a 'little trifling visit from Mr Fowke of 5 minutes'. Walsh complained that he knew as little of Margaret 'as if she was still in Benares' and that she was 'as usual prodigiously close as to revealing herself'.

Originally Margaret had considered holding the ceremony at Englefield House in the presence of Lady Clive, as advised by Walsh, but she chose instead to be married in St James's Church in London and Walsh refused to attend. Margaret cried during the ceremony as a consequence. Only a small group of friends and family were present: Francis (of course), Mr and Mrs Robinson (see page 133, friends of Benn's uncle Dr Brownrigg), Clive's son George, cousin William Holland, Lord and Lady Abergavenny (Lady Abergavenny was John Robinson MP's daughter), and a few others. Francis provided his sister with a dowry of £7,000 to which she added £3,000 of her own.

The older generation continued to cause problems. Francis had arranged a small pension for his father before he left India. Not that Joseph was entirely grateful, writing from Calcutta:

> ... *the annuity you propose to purchase for me is ample, and I have no fault to find with it, but that it has not come freely and with grace ...*[174]

The problem seems to have been that Joseph saw his own and his son's affairs as very closely entwined. It was due to Joseph's friendship with General Clavering that Francis had first been appointed Resident at Benares at a time when he, Joseph, was being proposed as Governor of Madras by Walsh. Joseph believed that Francis had risen as a result of his influence although, in reality, he had benefitted more from the influence of Walsh. Soon Joseph lost what little gratitude he had originally achieved and threatened to publish a letter describing Francis's ill treatment of him:

> *The enclosed I intend as a circular letter to all my acquaintances ... as you have shown so glaring a distrust of my honour, and have declined giving me so insignificant proof of your duty – as becoming a very distant security for ten thousand pounds ... I am at length obliged ... to throw off all future reliance on you.*[175]

---

[174] EUR, Kaye: Minor Collections, Fowke Mss: p 147: Joseph Fowke to his son Frank, Calcutta, end 1786.

[175] EUR, Kaye: Minor Collections, Fowke Mss: p 153: Joseph Fowke to son Frank Calcutta, 4 October 1786.

Joseph's ingratitude bordered on the psychotic. As we have seen, Joseph left India in 1788, two years after Francis and Margaret. Before he left, he arranged with Francis for Francis's half-sister, Sophia, to go out to India to seek a husband. Sophia, you will remember, was Joseph's daughter by Kitty Treacher and she had been brought up in Malmesbury by Joseph's younger brother Francis. Francis (son) had followed his father's wishes and had paid for Sophia's passage and for her upkeep at a cost of £2,000. Sophia was 'mad to go' although there were doubts as to whether she should. Her sister Louisa had died in 1784, aged fourteen, and her only protector during her childhood had been Francis the elder. Francis had raised her at Malmesbury and sent her to school in Cirencester, where Elizabeth Walsh, then Margaret Clive, had gone to school a generation earlier.

*Sophy has signified her consent joyously to go to India … I am seriously afraid the girl will lose her senses, and consequently think her by no means a fit person to be sent and recommended to India … some of her school companions have vilely insulted her with the meanness of her birth…[176]*

Life was not easy for Sophia due to her mother's questionable reputation but she was at least legitimate. 'Betsy', Joseph's daughter with Grace Crofts, (Margaret, Betsy, Sophia, and Louisa in that order) did not have that badge of respectability. Francis senior was prepared to help her but only so far. Shortly after Joseph returned to England in 1788 Joseph visited Malmesbury and Francis senior wrote to Francis junior about how Joseph wanted him to receive Betsy at home but this was going too far:

---

[176] EUR, Kaye: Minor Collections, Fowke Mss: p 163: Francis Fowke to his nephew Francis Fowke, Malmesbury 15 October 1787.

*[Joseph] ... wants me to receive Betsie but I refused ... but lo Betsy is going to live comfortably I hope with a husband, a Mr Patty, £200 a year etc ... how this will suit with your father I leave you to judge.*[177]

Francis junior helped Sophia financially with her journey to India but he appears not to have helped with letters of introduction, vital for anyone with any pretentions to respectability on first arrival. Those without letters of introduction were sometimes obliged to lodge in one of the many less than salubrious hotels of Madras or Calcutta, the resorts of sailors and others less savoury. Sophia must have had some introductions to make use of, from Joseph at least for what that might be worth, but within two years she was back in England complaining of lack of support from Francis, leading him to describe her as the least grateful of human beings.

Meanwhile, marriage to John Benn did nothing to deflect Margaret's musical ambitions. In May 1788, shortly after the first of her four miscarriages, she departed on a year's tour through Europe to Italy, where her intention was to play with 'finished' professional Italian musicians, then considered the best in the world. The logistics were impressive. It was vital that pianos awaited her at each stage of the route so that she could practise, and she wrote regular reports of her progress to Francis, from Brussels, Strasbourg and Zurich:

*I have been uninterruptedly engaged with my pianoforte. Benn told you that I practiced 4 hours a day but I can assure you I do nothing else the whole day through. I am mostly engaged in Haydn's music.*[178]

[177] Eur D456: Correspondence of the Fowke, Benn, Walsh and Maskelyne familes: Vol. 31, p 122: Francis Fowke (uncle) to Francis Fowke, Malmesbury 15 September 1788.

[178] Woodfield, Ian (2000): *Music of the Raj:* p 183: Margaret Fowke to Francis Fowke, Brussels 23 August 1788.

The piano had overtaken the harpsichord in the 1770s as the keyboard instrument of choice among young women. The surge in popularity started in 1768 when Johann Christian Bach, an international celebrity, played a new Zuppe piano at a concert for Queen Charlotte, wife of George III. Christian Bach was at that time Queen Charlotte's 'music master'. Margaret was a superb musician. In her father's words:

> I have not heard her equal among the foremost professors, either in delicacy of her touch or the variety of her sentiments.[179]

Once in Italy, she took lessons from some of those 'professors' and Italy was a triumph:

> The fame your sister has acquired in the musical world is very great. We have had many very pleasant concerts particularly in Rome. I think there is no fear at present of the death of the instrument [Margaret presumably] – it is so strongly nourished by praise'[180]

Francis and Benn were admiring and supportive, Francis playing down his own very considerable skill on the violin and cello. It was Francis whom Margaret turned to for advice on musical matters rather than the other way around. Despite her interest in mathematics, she never studied the theory of music so she was sometimes beholden to him for explanation of the finer points. She placed her emphasis on sensibility, evidenced by this letter to Warren Hastings of 1785:

> Indeed you are right in not regretting that you have never studied music … the power of music over a hearer certainly does not depend on knowledge, but upon a quick sensibility to a variety of emotions … You

---

[179] Eur D456: Correspondence of the Fowke, Benn, Walsh and Maskelyne familes: Vol. 30.

[180] Woodfield, Ian (2000): *Music of the Raj:* p 184: John Benn to Francis Fowke, Rome 17 February 1789.

*will see how little I respect musical knowledge when we meet – a distant day? – I will give you one more proof of how much I wish to make you my hearer tho' you do not possess it …*[181]

By early 1788, Francis had formed a relationship with a young woman called Mary Lowe. He was thirty-five and perhaps was ready for a more domestic life. There was a family of professional musicians called Lowe working in London at this date and it is probable that Mary was from that family. The liaison was in keeping with the times. From the 1770s, the social barrier between wealthy cognoscenti such as Francis and the professional musicians whom they employed began to blur, the musicians sometimes staying as guests with their patrons in their grand houses for weekends or longer. Although Margaret's son, Lord Ormathwaite, later described Mary Lowe as the 'daughter of a blacksmith' and as having been previously 'on the town', she was actually literate and educated and she suited Francis very well. Lord Ormathwaite was an unpleasant man and a snob. She had a cousin or second cousin, Richard Davis of Oxford, who was a gentleman and in the habit of taking a house in Brighton in the season.[182] While the Benns were 'honeymooning' on the continent, Francis and Mary set up house together in Mount Street, Mayfair.

Meanwhile the Man of Many Conflicts continued to cause difficulties. He was in need of money. By April 1789, he had fallen out with John Walsh again and that October he wrote to Francis, refusing to give up gambling completely in return for a pension:

*Avarice has taken too fast a hold of you to admit the power of truth … I will suffer death sooner than part one tittle from my right to your*

---

[181] Woodfield, Ian (2000): *Music of the Raj:* p125-6.

[182] Eileen and Harry Green (1973): *The Fowkes of Boughrood Castle*: p 3.

*original promise of a pension to me of £500 a year for life unconditional ... I will be trifled with no longer.* [183]

A week later he was up to his old technique, threatening to publish Francis's correspondence. Francis wrote to his uncle:

*What you would once have thought of the man who used this language after twice gaming away a fortune whilst he had at each time a different infant family depending on him ... his daughter (Sophia), the most ungrateful person that in all my intercourse with the world I have ever met.* [184]

And damningly to his father:

*The extreme contempt with which I view your threat of publication ... You will recollect that you gamed away your whole original fortune that, in consequence, the expence of mine, my brother Arthur's & Mrs Benn's education devolved upon my uncle Walsh, that I have repaid Mr Walsh for my share of it ... that afterwards in India whilst you had an infant family dependant upon you, you gamed away between five and six thousand pounds, that I left you with in India a bond for ten thousand rupees which you sold and spent – that I have been at the expence of about two thousand pounds in sending to India your natural daughter (Sophia), that I supported my Sister in India & portioned her on her marriage.* [185]

Perhaps Joseph was suffering some sort of breakdown. He replied:

*I received your mean and unmanly letter ... that I will not yield my right and that I spurn, however necessitous, the disgraceful offers you have*

---

[183] EUR, Kaye: Minor Collections, Fowke Mss: p 176, n 92: Joseph Fowke to Francis Fowke, Malmesbury 19 October 1789.

[184] EUR, Kaye: Minor Collections, Fowke Mss: p 176, n 93: Francis Fowke to Francis Fowke, Malmesbury October 1789.

[185] EUR, Kaye: Minor Collections, Fowke Mss: p 176, n 95: Francis Fowke to Joseph Fowke, October 1789.

*made me .. I shall hasten the publication of the wrongs you have done me.*[186]

He had a stroke later in the year. It was sad. As Margaret put it: 'an unjust quarrel with an only son seems to be the natural conclusion to my father's restless, turbulent, eccentric life'.[187] Fortunately, Francis junior was not one to hold a grudge, least of all against his own father and continued to harbour some affection, writing to his uncle that November:

*It is a pity that his abilities have always had that portion of genius & wildness which disqualify him for common life.*[188]

On their return from the Continent in 1789, after Margaret had suffered a second miscarriage in Plombieres which delayed their return home, the Benns set up house in Leatherhead and the following year 1790, Francis and Mary Lowe set up house in Wimbledon, where they lived for the next twenty-seven years, until 1817. The 'Roundhouse', where they lived and brought up their brood of nine children and Francis's Indian-born son William during the school holidays – William was educated at Francis's old school of Cheam - was demolished in the 1920s. There is only a small photo of it in Wimbledon Museum but a house of identical design is still standing [see picture].

Life for brother and sister was comfortably cushioned by Indian wealth. The letters that passed back and forth between them describe lives that were typically eighteenth-century but they were also surprisingly modern figures. Their level of wealth and leisure

---

[186] EUR, Kaye: Minor Collections, Fowke Mss: p 177, n 95: Joseph Fowke to his son, Francis Fowke, 29 October 1789.

[187] Eur D456: Correspondence of the Fowke, Benn, Walsh and Maskelyne familes: Vol. 11, p 77.

[188] EUR, Kaye: Minor Collections, Fowke Mss: p 177, n 95: Francis Fowke to Francis Fowke, November 1789.

ensured for them a style of life was in many ways similar to that of modern, early retirees, in that they had leisure and comfort but had to fill their days. The contexts are different but they would not seem very alien to their descendants in the twenty-first century if they were able to meet. There were walking trips in the West Country and elsewhere for Margaret and John Benn, visits to relations, visits to spa towns such as Bath and resorts such as Brighton, and, as ever, there was music and music theory, private concerts as well as public performances:

*Mon Trés Cher,*

*We have engaged Dussek & Raimonde to perform in Harley Street next Thursday evening .. I hope you will make us happy by joining us. We have only invited the Hollands & Stracheys as I wish to give a good deal of attention to Dussek's play, which a larger party would interrupt.*[189]

*My Dear Sister,*

*As you have made it a particular request, I have burnt your little dissertation on the mode of E minor & the imperfect chord – Tho I think you are perfectly right in your opinions ...*[190]

They discussed the great events of the day, in particular the French Revolution. The Fowkes were supportive and even when news of the Terror filtered back to England, Margaret was reluctant to question the intentions of the revolutionaries, being sympathetic to the extreme behaviour that poverty and fear can lead men to, although her sympathy was eventually tempered by horror at the excesses of the Terror.

---

[189] Private collection of Francis Fowke *Letters, Margaret Benn Walsh to Francis Fowke, 1790-1803, no 44,* to Wimbledon, Wednesday morning, 30 December 1791.

[190] Eur D456: Correspondence of the Fowke, Benn, Walsh and Maskelyne familes: Vol. 29, p 23: Francis Fowke to sister Margaret Benn-Walsh, Worthing 1 July 1812.

*... I have a very great desire to know what you think of French politics – It seems to me to be the fashion to run down the patriotic party in France. I feel there is a great deal of patriotism, moderation, heroic courage, & intelligence in the French nation at large ...[191]*

*What a dreadful degree of anarchy seems to prevail at this moment in France ... I look upon those horrible excesses to be the acts of an enraged populace, rendered still more cruel by artful unprincipled men who are always to be found in every country during great convulsions.[192]*

Life was not always easy. Margaret suffered from multiple stillbirths, writing to Francis from Margate in 1791:

*My dear Brother I am now grown familiar with my misfortune – I think my grief is wearing off ... but Objects do not look the same, Music does not sound the same – and Books are uninteresting ... whatever point of view I consider this fatal tendency in my constitution, it fills me with apprehension & horror – my fortitude is severely tried by seeing the tenderest hopes lost in the severest tortures – yet this is not all – the most alarming situations are often the consequence of bearing a dead child – I do not fear death unaccompanied by such horrifying circumstances.[193]*

*My character has undergone a thorough change by the bitter disappointments I have experienced. All that vehemence in my nature which at least indicated a capacity for happiness is quite gone – nothing now can interest me deeply. The pleasures of life present themselves to my imagination like the faintest sketches of a recollected dream. However differently you and I think on the subject of religion ... I will not scruple*

[191] Private collection of Francis Fowke *Letters, Margaret Benn Walsh to Francis Fowke, 1790-1803, no 40,* from Atherston, 20 August 1792.

[192] Private collection of Francis Fowke *Letters, Margaret Benn Walsh to Francis Fowke, 1790-1803, no 37,* to Wimbledon from Atherstone, 26 September 1792.

[193] Private collection belonging to Francis Fowke of *Letters, Margaret Benn Walsh to Francis Fowke, 1790-1803: no 51,* 15 February 1791.

*to tell you that the only consolation I have received in these cruel situations has been drawn from that source.[194]*

In 1794 after suffering the last of four miscarriages, Margaret gave birth to her first child, a girl. The following year, Francis's eldest boy, William, died at Wimbledon but by that time he and Mary Lowe had produced the first four of their fifteen children, of whom eleven survived to adulthood. Their house was full of the sound of music and young voices. Francis delighted in his family and was apparently 'shy in large society when not well acquainted' and 'music occupied much of his time'.[195] He was also interested in shorthand, which he taught himself. He was in general averse to public service although he became commander of the Wimbledon light horse volunteers.

John Walsh died at his house in Chesterfield Street on 1st March 1795. He had become increasingly 'irritable, capricious and tyrannical'[196] and had fallen out with Francis and disinherited him, perhaps because Francis allowed Mary Lowe, to take his name.[197] After disinheriting Francis, Walsh then intended to bequeath his fortune to Clive's former secretary Sir Henry Strachey but got into a flaming argument with Strachey about Samuel Johnson during what should have been a convivial dinner at Walsh's Mayfair residence. Strachey admired Johnson but Walsh detested him, sneeringly referring to him as 'the great moralist'. Margaret attempted to mediate between dining room and parlour and the row appeared to have ended amicably but several days later Walsh changed his will, leaving everything to Margaret in trust for her

---

[194] Private collection belonging to Francis Fowke of *Letters, Margaret Benn Walsh to Francis Fowke, 1790-1803: no 53:* to No 2 Picadilly, from Margate, 1791 Thursday.

[195] Mss Eur 032, *Memoir of Margaret Elizabeth Benn-Walsh (née Fowke).*

[196] Mss Eur 032, *Memoir of Margaret Elizabeth Benn-Walsh (née Fowke).*

[197] Mss Eur 032, *Memoir of Margaret Elizabeth Benn-Walsh (née Fowke).*

eldest son (then unborn), conditional on a name change from Benn to Benn-Walsh.

The whole of Walsh's estate therefore went to Margaret and her husband provided they changed their name, which they did, and the Benn-Walshes moved from Leatherhead to Warfield Park, reluctantly on Margaret's part since it was the scene of unhappy childhood memories, an aversion that Francis advised to her to overcome:

> *I well know the acuteness of your feelings, that words can do little to mitigate or soften them & that time is the only God (speaking as a heathen) that can afford you relief – yet you must use a little honest hypocracy & not increase your mate's suffering by discovering an unconquerable aversion to the place …[198]*

Margaret offered to share her inheritance with Francis but he refused although he accepted half the income from it for life. It was the injection of this additional money from John Walsh's estate that enabled John Benn-Walsh and Francis to purchase land in Radnorshire. That same year, 1795, Francis became High Sheriff of Radnorshire but he declined to become a Tory MP and to purchase a baronetcy, saying he would 'rather have a good quartet' - although perhaps the expense and the work were uninviting to a man who was already father to several children. It was John Benn-Walsh who purchased a baronetcy, naming it 'Ormathwaite' after his birthplace in the Lake District.

John Walsh is buried in St Michael's Church Warfield. His memorial, a large bas-relief figure of a 'Sorrowing Maiden', is on the south wall, with words written by Margaret beneath. Joseph Fowke lived on, mainly in Bath, and money continued to be tight.

---

[198] Eur D456: Correspondence of the Fowke, Benn, Walsh and Maskelyne familes: Vol. 28, p 29: Francis Fowke to Margaret Benn-Walsh, Hertford Str. 23 February 1809.

In 1791, Edmund Burke had raised Joseph's case in Parliament, urging the Directors of the Company to grant him a lump sum of £1,700, which, typically, he turned down as insufficient. His relationship with Francis continued to be difficult:

*you reply ... with the most deliberate insensibility and cruelty ... I shall make no alterations in my present parsimonious way of life ... You may break my heart but you shall never bend it ... learn to despise as you ought to do, the scandalous and mean declaration of your cousin William Holland.[199]*

Once John Walsh was gone there were few of Joseph's generation left. His sister Sophia had died in Calcutta in 1760 and his older brother Edward died in 1789. There was only his younger brother Francis, still living in Malmesbury and still a benign figure. Joseph became deaf and needed an ear-trumpet, which must have been hard for someone so passionately interested in music, as Beethoven would later testify, but he evidently 'retained the vigour of his intellects until the close of his life and what perhaps is more remarkable, wrote, till his death, 'a hand of singular firmness and beauty'. The activity of his mind and the liveliness of imagination remained to the last'.[200] He died in Bath on 16th May 1800, bequeathing to the sole beneficiary of his will 'a debt due to me from the East India Company of which I have been unjustly deprived'.[201]

Back in Wimbledon, Francis and Mary had a new baby almost every year. The two eldest boys, Francis and John, went to Eton and Francis, the eldest, played the violin and the organ and was a very keen musician like his father.

---

[199] EUR, Kaye: Minor Collections, Fowke Mss: p 105: Joseph Fowke to his son Francis, Canterbury 4 March 1793.

[200] *Gentleman's Magazine*, 87, Part 2, p.527-8.

[201] *Dictionary of National Biography*, Joseph Fowke.

*I am near having a flogging. I shall be much obliged if you will send me some more duets ...[202]*

Francis Fowke and Mary Lowe were eventually married at Gretna Green in 1801. The reason for the secrecy was no doubt that they did not want it to be widely known that they had been living unwed for many years and this was Francis making an honest woman of Mary, no doubt at her request. It was an ill-thought-out act however, because they went on to have further children after 1801 and those later children were born *within* wedlock whereas the older children were not and therefore the elder children were effectively disinherited. On 9th July 1813, when Francis was sixty and after all his children had been born, they got married for a second time, in what might be described as 'self-bigamy', and it was this second marriage which was noted in Francis's will, where he specifically testifies that the marriage took place after all their eleven surviving children had been born, thus delegitimising all of them equally.

The older children sometimes stayed at Warfield Park with the Benn-Walshes but their uncertain legal status may have cast a cloud.[203] Around 1815, Francis was somehow persuaded that a country estate was necessary for a man of his social standing even though social standing had never been among his highest priorities. In 1816/17 he started work on the building of Boughrood Castle, not a castle but a new build with the ruins of a medieval castle in the grounds, which were useful as a folly or a conversation point.

*It has been with much hesitation & reluctance that I have engaged in building, to which I ever had an utter dislike ... However there are advantages in being on one's own land – but it is useless now to discuss*

[202] EUR, Kaye: Minor Collections, Fowke Mss: p 207, 11F: Francis cFowke to his father Francis Fowke, Eton 26 May 1801.

[203] Eileen and Harry Green (1973): *The Fowkes of Boughrood Castle*: p 2.

*the matter as the house will be roofed in a few weeks, which is wonderfully expeditious ... The spot is extremely beautiful more so on the whole I think than even this – but I have little relish for the change ... Sir Charles Morgan has, in a very obliging manner, offered me a house in that neighbourhood which he has lately quitted ... I shall send down for my furniture from town.*[204]

While supervising the building of Boughrood Castle the Fowkes rented neighbouring Dderw Mansion. They moved into their new home sometime in 1817/18 but Francis had little time to enjoy it; he died on 12th October 1819 at the age of sixty-six, analytical to the last:

*I do not recollect that before my last illness I thought myself in immediate danger, and in this situation I experienced a sentiment that was also quite new to me – the road back to health seemed so beset with pain, languor & suffering that it appeared almost a question whether one might not as well continue on that road to termination at which we must ultimately arrive.*[205]

He is buried at Boughrood.

Mary lived on until 1847, at Boughrood for most of that time. She had aged into a large corpulent woman, hard to avoid after so many births, but she was a loving mother, as is reflected in the correspondence. But sadly, the correspondence loses vitality as the new century progresses, as if the correspondents were slowly suffocating beneath a blanket of Victorian propriety. Terms of endearment become more formulaic, sentiments more predictable.

---

[204] Eur D456: Correspondence of the Fowke, Benn, Walsh and Maskelyne familes: Vol. 12, p 140: Francis Fowke to Margaret Benn-Walsh, St Mary's Church. 16 October 1817.

[205] Eur D456: Correspondence of the Fowke, Benn, Walsh and Maskelyne familes: Vol. 28, p 152: Francis Fowke to Margaret Benn-Walsh, Half Moon 6 November 1819.

In addition, there was disagreement. The difficulties created by Francis's will festered for years. In it, as we have seen, he deliberately delegitimised all his children by dating his marriage to Mary *after* all their children had been born. One granddaughter even worked briefly as a servant in the house that her grandfather had built. When it was all over and the court cases finally wound up, each of the nine children inherited £2,235, the final disbursement being in 1836. This was a sum equivalent to £245,000 at today's value, a large sum but far from the great wealth created, squandered or inherited by the three previous generations. The disputes between the siblings are well described in Eileen and Harry Green's booklet, included here as an appendix, and are beyond the remit of the present account.

# Appendix I
## The Descendants of Francis Fowke and Mary Lowe
### Copied from The Fowkes of Boughrood Castle
### by Harry & Eileen Green

**F**rancis Fowke 1789-1826: b. St. George's. Hanover Square, probably in Mount Street; educated at Eton (Oppidan); he played the violin and organ. In 1806 he went to Madras as a cavalry cadet in the H.E.I.C. forces, but resigned for health reasons. He was "much above six feet", but not robust. His father then bought him a cornetcy (later, a lieutenancy) in the 14th Light Dragoons, and he served in Portugal, Spain and France till 1814. He was wounded before Salamanca but returned to his regiment in time to take part in the assault, July 22, 1812. After his father's death, he bought a captaincy in his regiment, but went on half-pay immediately. As an Overseer of the Poor, he sent his butler to represent him at Vestry meetings. He was responsible for major alterations to the exterior and interior of Boughrood Castle, and left debts of £4,473-1-3 at his death. He was unmarried but had acknowledged illegitimate issue,

James Francis Fowke, b.1822, by Ann Phillips, Llanfillo, Breconshire.

**Henry Fowke** b.1790 at St. Marylebone; d.at Wimbledon, 1793.

**Mary Fowke** (1792-): b. Wimbledon. Educated by governess, tutors and her father: she could read Italian and "accompany a concert or trio with the thro' bass in a very respectable way".[206] Mary married twice: (1) 1811 John Watts (d. 1815), a native of Battle, Sussex, and an attorney at Worthing, who was ruined by his association with unsuccessful property speculators, and had issue,

---

[206] Bundle 27, F.51, Ormathwaite Collection

Francis (1S13-1839), Emily, who reached the age of 21 but died unmarried before 1850, and James Alexander (c. 1815-1825); (2) 1826, at Llyswen, Breconshire, when she was 34, David Lewis Williams, Gent. (c. 1806-1855), aged 21, and had issue Adelaide Mary (b. 1827), David Arthur (1829-1844), William Alfred (b. 1831), Frederick (b.1834), and Henry Edward.

Mary's unscrupulous second husband was a descendant of David Williams, Y Gaer, Breconshire, High Sheriff of Breconshire, 1753, and son of the Rev. William Williams (c. 1776-1847), Rector of Llyswen. Immediately after his marriage, he matriculated at St. John's College, Cambridge, graduated, and was ordained. He and Mary lived at Cwmdu, Crickhowell, except when he was doing a nominal stint as a curate at Trinity Church, Ely, Cambridgeshire, 1850-51.[207] He became Rector of Llyswen in 1855, the year of his death. Understandably, both Mary and her husband lied to the Ely census enumerator about their age. Their second son, William Alfred, was appointed Second Master at Fauconbridge School, Beccles, Suffolk.

**John Fowke** (1794-1851): Born at Wimbledon and educated at Eton (Oppidan) where he was said to be so good-natured he could not keep a farthing in his pocket—he got into debt through treating his school-mates. His father bought him an ensigncy in the 68th Regiment of Foot in 1812, and he served in the Peninsular War. He was wounded at Vitoria and got great credit for remaining on the ground and encouraging his men. His father bought him a lieutenancy and he served in Ireland till 1818, when he went on half-pay. He sold out before 1844.

---

[207] Parish registers, searched by Mr. Reginald Holmes, Ely; A4 Curates' Papers, Ely Episcopal Records, Cambridge University Library, searched by Mr. Peter Rushton, John's College, Cambridge.

He married three times: (1) 1822 at Belfast, Jane Ferguson (d. 1828), daughter of John Stevenson Ferguson, and had issue Francis (1823-1865); and John Stevenson Ferguson (b. 1825). (2) Esther Heany, in Ireland, and had issue Henry Heany (1839-1873); Jane (b.1841); and Esther Julia Mary (1842-1886). (3) 1846, at Newcastle-on-Tyne, Jane Borthwick (1823-1887), daughter of Thomas Borthwick, a shipwright, and had issue William (b.1848); and John (1851-1939). Jane Borthwick was illiterate.

Lt. Fowke's eldest son by his first marriage, Col. Francis Fowke, R.E.,[208] was a distinguished military engineer, an inventor, and the original designer of the Albert Hall rotunda. He married, at St. Marylebone, Louisa Charlotte Rede, daughter of the Rev. Robert Rede Rede, of Beccles. Col. Fowke's second son, Frank Rede Fowke (1847-1927) was educated at Eton and became Assistant Secretary to the Board of Education, and Secretary to the Committee on Solar Physics. He presented the Fowke Mss. to the India Office Library. He married Isabella Langdale Cole, daughter of Sir Henry Cole, K.C.B., and had issue: Joyce Audrey Rede, who married Lt. Col. Count Stanislas Julien Ignatius Ostrorog; Lettice Joan Rede, who married Jean Baptiste Thomas Douay; and Olive Summerley Rede, who married Andre Louis Mangeot (1883-1970), the concert violinist, and had issue: Fowke J. A. Mangeot (Company Director),[209] and Silvain Mangeot (Foreign Service).

---

[208] 76 See D.N.B. Col. Fowke appears to have inherited some of the peculiar qualitiesof his paternal grandfather, who invented a form of shorthand (500 of the Fowke Mss. are written in it) and suggested to the Government the use of land-lighthouses for signalling.

[209] Mr. Mangeot was trained as a Chartered Accountant (a profession in which three of his Walsh ancestors were trained) and then became the Financial Director of a company in the G.E.C. Group, specializing in airborne electronics.

Lt. Fowke's second son by his first marriage, Major John Stevenson Ferguson Fowke, served with the 54th West Norfolk Regiment of Foot from 1842 to 1868.

Henry Heany Fowke, a wharfinger's clerk who became a merchant, married Mary Ann Bruce, daughter of David Bruce, a Newcastle ship- owner, and had issue John Francis (1866-1943). David Bruce and others. Because of his father's early death, John Francis Fowke, was an office boy in a ship-owner's office at the age of 13, but became a shorthand writer, a chartering clerk and eventually the general manager. He married and had one daughter, Estella Walwyn (Mrs. Clifford Howes Carey). Henry Heany Fowke's half-brother, John Fowke, was a solicitor's clerk in 1878; in his will, signed in 1932, he styles himself "John Fowke Gentleman". He married and had four daughters and three sons.

**Richard Fowke** (1795-1855): b. St. George's, Hanover Square; educated at Baling Great School (headmaster, Dr. Geo. Nicholas); entered the Royal Navy in 1806, as a midshipman, and served for three years in the Mediterranean; in 1809, he joined the flagship, "Barfleur", and from 1812, the 38-gun frigate, "Menelaus", Captain Sir Peter Parker, distinguishing himself in small-boat actions by coolness under galling fire, and disgracing himself ashore by dissolute habits. At one point, Parker asked Francis Fowke to remove his sons because of Richard's behaviour, but the difficulty was resolved; after a spell on the "Vengeur", 74 guns, Richard joined the Sloop "Linnet", 16 guns, and saw fierce action on Lake Champlain in the American War 1812-14; the "Linnet", Captain Daniel Pring, distinguished herself in the Lake action, part of the Battle of Plattsburgh (September 11, 1814), but was forced to strike her colours because the British squadron had surrendered. Ten of her complement were killed, including Richard's midshipman messmate, and fourteen wounded. Richard was mentioned in Captain Pring's despatch, and was well treated in his short captivity.

After the war, and promotion to Lieutenant (1816), he served in the Coast Blockade (depot ship, "Talavera") and guard ships. Of his naval service, 14 years were on full pay, and 27 on half-pay. He married before 1838, Mary, daughter of Mrs. Margaret Clarke, a substantial property owner of Pont-y-wal House, Bronllys, Breconshire. They had no issue, and Mary died, aged 86, in 1886. Their home had been in Hugh Street, Pimlico (miscalled High Street in Fowke v. Fowke.).

**Henrietta Fowke** (1796-): b. St. George's, Hanover Square. After girlhood, in which there are glimpses of her in amateur dramatics or transcribing letters into the shorthand which her father invented, Henrietta, a typical Victorian maiden aunt, makes only fugitive appearances, and always in other people's lives; even her given name is a shadow of a dead brother, Henry. In the 1830s, she is at Boughrood, pressing the claims of Mary to a greater share of the estate. In 1850, she is living with Philip Fowke and his family at Picton Terrace, Carmarthen. Next year, still unmarried, she is in Cologne with Sunderland and Robert.

**Sunderland Clay Fowke** (1798-1873): b. St. George's, Hanover Square; educated at Great Baling School. He entered the Royal Navy as a midshipman in 1812, with an allowance of £40 a year from his father (Francis junior, in the cavalry, needed £200). In 1813, he joined the "Menelaus" in which Richard was serving, took part in unsuccessful hunting of American frigates in the Atlantic by a flying squadron, and then went ashore with the naval forces attacking Washington. As a very junior aide-de-camp, he watched the burning of the White House and the Capitol. With no prospects of promotion after the end of the Napoleonic and

American Wars, he left the Navy without taking his lieutenancy examination.

He was living at Llandevilog House, Breconshire with his mother, shortly before, and for some time after, his brother Francis's death. With his brother Edward, he negotiated the unsuccessful and successful sales of the Fowke estate, and, as the senior resident son at Boughrood Castle in the 1830s, he carried most of the family troubles on his shoulders and also felt, as a property owner, the weight of what he called "these distressing and dangerous times"; his relaxations were angling and netting in the Wye; the season at Tenby; and yachting in the Bristol Channel. From 1830 to 1834, he courted Ann Llewellin Price, of St. Julian's House, Tenby, orphan daughter of Peter Price, and granddaughter of Peter Price, senior, a self-made Tenby master-builder and merchant.

The marriage took place in 1834 at Tenby. Sunderland and Ann lived near his mother in the terrace known as Little Paragon, but Ann died in childbirth in 1837. Issue: Mary Fanny Price (b. 1836); and Ann Jane Price (1837-1864). Mary married W. T. Holland, pottery manufacturer, Llanelli, and had one son, William Sutherland, who died in infancy. Sunderland left Tenby after 1841, lived at one time at Glanhenwy with his brother Edward at Cologne, in London, and eventually at Gunfort Terrace, Tenby, with his brother Philip's widow and her daughter Laura, a governess. He died in Cornwall in 1873.

**Edward Fowke** (1800-1872): b. St. George's, Hanover Square, educated at Great Ealing School. After an abortive exercise in trade, at Corfu, he became a tenant farmer at the Lodge, Talgarth, Breconshire, and agent for the Breconshire estates of the Earl of Ashburnham. He was later the agent for the Maesllwch Estate and lived at Glanhenwy, near Hay. For the greater part of his professional life he was agent for the Glanusk Estate and lived at

Penmyarth, Breconshire. He was one of the valuers when Boughrood Tithe Map was made. In 1831 he married Mrs. Elizabeth Forrester, a draper's widow and daughter of Evan and Joan Prosser of Tredustan Court and Porthamel, landed proprietors with several High Sheriffs in the family tree. Issue: Elizabeth (d.i.i.); Edward (1834-1854); Sarah (b. 1836); Francis (1838-1859) who entered the Bombay Civil Service and died of fever soon after his arrival; and Ada (b. 1841).

Acknowledged illegitimate issue: Edward (b. 1827) by Mary Nott, a housemaid at Boughrood Castle, who was pregnant by Edward when she witnessed the death-bed will of his brother Francis. Mary Nott had two other bastard children: John (b. 1818); and Elizabeth (b. 1823), who describes herself as Elizabeth Fowke, Independent, in the Talgarth census return of 1841. Mary Nott's relations with the Fowke sons appear to have been complex.

**Robert Fowke**: b. 1801, St. George's. Hanover Square. He appears to have had no profession. As a young man, he was much at Tenby, where he was interested in Elizabeth Sleeman, niece of Captain (later General) Sleeman, the destroyer of Thuggee. She was not interested in Robert. He married Isabella, in or about 1836, and lived at Llan-pwll-llyn, Boughrood (now known as the Old Vicarage). Isabella died in child-birth, 1837. Issue: Robert (1837-1879), who became a solicitor at Brecon, and is listed in 1873 as owning 107 acres of land (gross estimated rent, £126) in Radnorshire. Robert Fowke the elder, like Sunderland, appears to have been a wandering widower, who at one time found Cologne a cheap, genteel haven.

**Philip Fowke** (1802-1852): b. St. George's, Hanover Square. He married at Tenby, 1842, Francis Anne Baker, daughter of Edward Jordan Baker, Gent., and had issue Mary Frances (b. 1845); Emily Elizabeth (b. 1845); Philip Francis (b. 1846);

Richardson William (b. 1847), all at Carmarthen; Jane (b. 1850); and Laura (1850), at Notting Hill. He was a school proprietor at Picton Terrace, Carmarthen, till 1850, and his widow was keeping a boarding school for young ladies in Lansdowne Crescent, Notting Hill, in 1861. She had retired to a cottage in Gunfort Terrace, Tenby, by 1871. See Sunderland Clay Fowke.

Philip also had an illegitimate son, Philip Probert Fowke (b. 1827), by Mary Probert of Nantmel, Radnorshire, a servant at Boughrood Castle.[210] This boy was himself a servant, aged 14, in the household of Henry Proctor, surgeon. Broad Street, Hay, in 1841.

**Emily Fowke** (1804-1807): baptised Emmeline, at St. George's, Hanover Square, but never referred to by that name. Her death seems to have had an unforgettable effect on the family.

**Charles Fowke** (1805-1882): b. St. George's, Hanover Square. Farmer at Newhouse, Llanstephan, and elsewhere, land surveyor. He formed an association with and may have married Anne Prosser (1807-1853) of Newhouse Farm. They had issue: Charles Edward (b. 1826), illegitimate; Ann (b. 1828); Eliza Amelia (b.1830); Mary Eliza (b. 1832); Edward (b. 1835); Robert (b. 1836); Isabella (b. 1838); Henry (b. 1839); Matilda (b. 1840); Francis Arthur (b. 1840, d.i.i.); Elizabeth Julia (b. 1844); Blanche Laura (b. 1847).

The eldest son, Charles Edward, a sailor, married Margaret, a dressmaker, and lived at Tenby; issue: Thomas (b. 1848), a sailor; Charles Edward (b. 1849); Sarah Jane (b. 1853); and John Nicholls (b. 1860). Charles's second daughter, Eliza Amelia, married Acting Lt. Herbert Thomas Ryves, R.N., at Llyswen, Breconshire, in 1849.

---

[210] Information: Mr. D. Emrys Williams.

Ryves served as Chief Officer of an H.E.I.C. war-steamer in the first Opium War, and was severely wounded at Amoy. He was a Senior Lieutenant in the R.N. in the River Plate, 1844-1847, and was later a Coast Guard officer. He retired with the rank of Commander in 1866 and lived at St. Asaph, Flintshire, and at Denbigh. He and Eliza Amelia had one child, Emma Fanny, who married Pierce Hugh Pierce of St. Asaph.

In 1850, Charles Fowke petitioned in Chancery for a greater share in his father's estate, but the action was dismissed for want of prosecution, and Charles was ordered to pay costs. He was an inmate of Hay Union Workhouse in 1861. Five years later, he emigrated to Braidwood, N.S.W., with his daughter Matilda and his carpenter son, Edward, and Edward's wife and children.[211] Edward became a bush farmer. His daughter, Elizabeth Jane, married Alfred Robertson,[212] a bush farmer; their daughter, Ellen Robertson, married a Braidwood grazier, Edward Bunn, and had five children, one of whom is Dr. Terence A. Bunn, of Thirroul, N.S.W. Dr. Bunn married Zilla Madrell, of Braidwood; they had seven children.

---

[211] Edward Fowke (1835-1909) married twice: (1) Jane Anna Morgan Ashfield, at Roath, Cardiff, 1858, and had issue: Anna Elizabeth Jane, 1860, in Swansea; Charles Edward, (1863) (d.i.i.?), at Paddington Charles, 1865; and Edward (1868); (2) Elizabeth Townsend, at Braidwood, N.S.W. and had issue, in Sydney: Isabella; Francis; Robert; Verbina; Georgina; Frederick Herbert; and a son and a daughter who died before 1909. Information: Dr. Terenee A. Bunn.

[212] Though Robertson's poor farm lay in bush so thick that he had to blaze a trail for his children to the school at Bendoura, all his children were taught to play a musical instrument; and so were the children of Mrs. Ellen (Robertson) Bunn. This was a Fowke tradition: Joseph, his son Francis, and his grandson Capt. Francis, all took violins or a cello, or both, to India; Margaret Fowke, in India, collected native airs. Francis Fowke and his thirteen surviving bastards could have formed an orchestra—with mother playing the harp.

**Frederick Fowke** (1807-1863): b. St. George's, Hanover Square. Medical practitioner, licensed at Apothecaries Hall, 1833, and admitted a Member of the Royal College of Surgeons, 1834. He lived and practised in Berkeley Square until 1856, when he moved to Bonchurch, Isle of Wight. He married Anne Wainwright (d. 1863), of Bristol, and had issue: Frederick (b. 1842), and Anne (b. 1845).

**Elizabeth Fowke** (1809-1882): b. Grove House, Hampton, Middlesex, a twin. Educated at C. Clarke's Boarding School. She married, 1830, at Lydd, Kent, Thomas Bell, surgeon, R.N. (1797-1854), and had issue Julia (b. 1831, Boughrood Castle); Frances; Alexander; George Nugent; Frederick; Francis; Edmund; Frances (d.i.i.); and Ellen (d.i.i.). The second and third children were probably born in London; the last six, at Braidwood, New South Wales. Thomas Bell (1797-1854) was the third son of George Bell, Gent., of Bellevue, Enniskillen, Co. Fermanagh, Ireland, who claimed descent from Edward the Elder, through Sir Robert Bell, Speaker of the House of Commons and Lord Chief Baron of the Exchequer who died in 1577. The Bells' holding was part of the Plantation of Ulster, and probably dated from the last quarter of the 17th Century. Thomas Bell's brothers were General Sir George Bell, who, as an Ensign, carried the colours at Badajoz, and Frederick Nugent Bell, genealogist and barrister, who is alleged to have been a government agent-provocateur before Peterloo; he died insolvent.

Thomas Bell entered the Royal Navy in 1822, and was assistant surgeon on the "Fury" in Parry's third expedition to the Arctic. The "Fury" was wrecked, and Bell returned on the "Hecla" in 1825, and was admitted a Member of the Royal College of Surgeons that year. He received his first Warrant as surgeon, R.N.. in 1827 and served in the East Indies before joining the "Talavera", at Sheerness, depot ship in the Coast Blockade, where he met Lt. Richard

Fowke. Between 1832 and 1838, he was surgeon-superintendent of three convict ships, the "Eliza", the "Portsea" and the "Prince George". Under a government scheme to create a magisterial land-owning class in New South Wales from experienced officers, he bought 760 acres of land at Braidwood for £40, rented 2,560 acres as a squatter, and built a house, "Bellevue", on his rented land, where he was joined by Elizabeth and her family in 1840. A second house, "Bendoura", on Bell's land, was burnt down by convicts with all his English furniture the night before it was to have been occupied. It was repaired as a one-storey house, and became the family home for three generations.

As a sheep-farmer, surgeon, Justice of the Peace, Commissioner of Crown Lands, and Anglo-Irish gentleman of the Anglican persuasion, he was a very important person in a small community which had brought with it all the social and religious distinctions of the United Kingdom (including Ireland), further complicated by distinctions between free settlers, convicts and emancipists, and enlivened by fierce quarrels over horse-racing. It only needed the Braidwood gold rush of 1852 (gold was found there first on Bell's rented land) and 5,000 miners to create a society in which even John Walsh would have had some difficulty in making fine moral and social distinctions. In spite of the gold, Bell made no fortune. His son Francis, succeeded him as a sheep farmer, but bad times came and the land was sold. Francis's daughter, Mrs. Frances Mary Harding, now aged 92, became a hospital sister, and now lives in Sydney with her daughter, Mrs. Beryl Corlette, whose husband is a medical practitioner. Two more generations are flourishing.

**Eliza Fowke** (1809-1849). Twin. Educated at C. Clarke's boarding school, where the joint fees for Elizabeth and Eliza were £59-15-0. She married, 1834, George Games, Gent., at Tenby, and lived with him at Boughrood Castle, and then at Llan-pwil-llyn, Boughrood, up to 1839, when Games became a farmer at

Glasbury, Radnorshire. Both died of typhus in 1849—Eliza in January and Games in February. Issue: Georgina Sarah (b. 1834); Eliza Isabella (b. 1837); and Anna Maria Hughes (b. 1839). Games was connected with the Talgarth, Breconshire Games, generally considered to have descended in the bastard line from Davy Gam. In the early nineteenth century most of them were craftsmen, but one strain was beginning to emerge into gentility and the landed and professional classes.

After the death of Eliza and George, their daughters were brought up at Brecon, first by their uncle, John Games, a builder, and then with their second cousin, William Games, attorney, who was three times Mayor of Brecon. Georgiana Sarah married her second cousin, George Games, solicitor, Hay, who owned 167 acres in Radnorshire, Breconshire, and Herefordshire (gross estimated rent £208) in 1873. Eliza Isabella described herself, grandly, as "landed proprietor" in the Brecon census return, 1861: while a blade of grass remained to produce rent, she rejected bourgeois status.

# Appendix II
## Who was Dr Edward Fowke of Cork?

There had been Fowkes in Ireland since the early seventeenth century when a Roger Fowke of Gunstone (1588-1649), which lies in the southern part of the parish of Breewood, Staffordshire, who had twenty children, went out with the first wave of Protestant settlers under James I/VI. His fifth son, Edward (1629-1689(?)), was possibly Randal's father. Alternatively, Frank Rede Fowke conjectures that Randal's father was an Edward Fowke (1623-1689(?)) son of Thomas Fowke of Breewood itself (1582-1642) and also mentioned in the Staffordshire Fowke genealogies. There are thus two Edwards, contemporaries and sixth cousins, who qualify for Dr Edward of Cork although Edward, son of Roger of Gunstone, seems the more likely: (See next page for tree.)

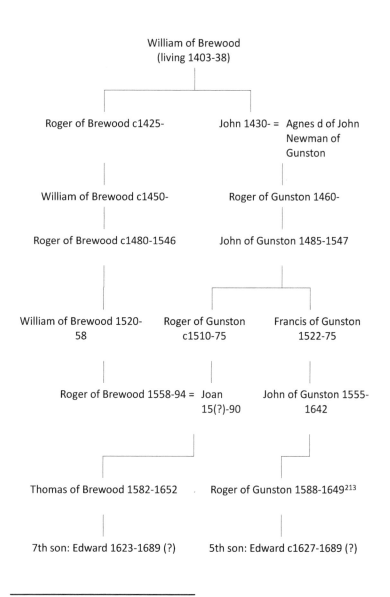

William of Brewood
(living 1403-38)

Roger of Brewood c1425-

John 1430- = Agnes d of John
Newman of
Gunston

William of Brewood c1450-

Roger of Gunston 1460-

Roger of Brewood c1480-1546

John of Gunston 1485-1547

William of Brewood 1520-58

Roger of Gunston c1510-75

Francis of Gunston 1522-75

Roger of Brewood 1558-94 = Joan 15(?)-90

John of Gunston 1555-1642

Thomas of Brewood 1582-1652

Roger of Gunston 1588-1649[213]

7th son: Edward 1623-1689 (?)

5th son: Edward c1627-1689 (?)

---

[213] The author Martha Fowke Sanson, 1689-1736, was a great-grandaughter of this Roger, 1588-1649. She learned to write by writing her father Philip's love letters. Philip was later murdered by his valet.

# Appendix III
## Will of Randal Fowke

IN THE NAME OF GOD AMEN I, RANDALL FOWKE OF FORT Sᵀ. GEORGE ON THE COAST OF CHORAMANDELL being at this present Writeing in a good state of health, with perfect mind and memory after giving my most humble, and hearty thanks to almighty God for the Enjoyment of the same; hopeing forgiveness of all my sins comitted against his Divine Majesty and the Errors of my Life past, and Redemption from the punishment due to them thrô the sufferings merits and mediation of my Blessed Lord and saviour JESUS CHRIST I now by his Grace call to mind the certainty of Death and the uncertain Time of it's approach for which reason, I do think it necessary to make my Last Will and Testament; And do now make it in manner and form following IN the first place, I will I Order, and do Direct, that all my Funeral Charges, just and Lawfull Debts and what Legacys and Bequests herein after mention'd be duly Discharged, and satisfied for the due performance of all which. and what more thing or things I shall or may hereafter think fit and proper to appoint and have done or Will Order or Direct, I do hereby Nominate, Ordain and Constitute my dear and Well beloved sons EDWARD FOWKE, JOSEPH FOWKE, and FRANCIS FOWKE Lawfull Executors to this my Last Will, and Testament Enjoining them strictly as it is their Duty to fulfill it in every article. *Imprimis* I do Give and Bequeath to my Beloved Cozen MARTHA ROGERS in Cork in Ireland, if alive one Year after my Decease, the sum of Thirty Pounds sterling but if she should be Defunct before the remittance of the said sum can reach her, I then and in such Case Will and Direct, that it Devolve to my Estate, and be accounted as part thereof. Item I Will and Bequeath to my very Loveing Friend the reverend Doctʳ. Charles Long Minister of Cheiveley in Berkshire the sum of Fifty Pounds sterling. and to his Wife Elizabeth, Twenty pounds sterling. ITEM I Give and Bequeath to Mʳˢ. Hannah Greenhaugh the sum of Thirty pagodas for Mourning. Item I Give and Bequeath to my friend Mʳ. Thomas Cooke the sum of One Hundred pagodas and to his Wife Mʳˢ. Grace Cook the sum of Thirty Pagodas for mourning. ITEM I do Give and Bequeath to my son in law Capᵗ. John Holland and to my Daughter Sophia his wife, and to their son Richard Holland to each of them the sum of One Hundred Pagodas. ITEM I do Give and Bequeath unto Mary Flora Daughter of Maria Flora deceas'd the small 'iouse situate in the Pedda Nagnes Petta in the Oilmaker's street, which I bought of Villante Harris as ₱ Bill of Sale Register'd bearing Date Janʳʸ. the 5ᵗʰ. 173⁵ doth more fully appear—I also Give and Bequeath to the said Mary Flora the sum of Five Hundred Pagodas to be pay'd unto her at the age of Twenty One years: (she being Born the 6ᵗʰ. day of February anno 1736/7) or the day of her marriage which shall first happen provided she spontaneously Embrace and profess the protestant Religion and continue in the same if otherwise, I do hereby Bequeath unto her no more than the sum of One hundred Pagodas. MOREOVER Dureing the time ere she arrives at the age of Twenty One Years, or the day of Marriage, I Will I order and do Direct that the sum of Five Pagodas be duly pay'd her the first day of every month after my Decease, for her Cloathing, and subsistance : also the further sum of Five Pagodas ₱ Month for her schooling and Education and for the due performing fulfilling and Discharging this Bequest now mentioned, I Will I order and do Direct that such a sufficient part of my Estate either in houses, Money, or other Effects shall be kept seperate, Deposited and secured in such manner as may be lawfully judged most proper on such occasion, or for such use and Behoof as of the said Mary Flora. MOREOVER for the due Executing of this part of my Last Will and Testament I do Desire and Charge my Dealy beloved sons and Executors aforenamed dureing her Orphan, or unmarry'd state to inquire and Examin frequently the person or persons who have or may have the Care of the said Mary Flora whether the said Monthly allowances be duly appropriated to the uses aforesaid and as Design'd; which, hope will be with all humanity and Charity, be Considered as reasonable. But in Case it should please God to take her out of this Life before the age of Twenty One Years or the Day of Marriage, My Will is and I do hereby order that the said Monthly allowances shall then Cease, and what I have herein bequeath'd her Devoire to my Estate and be accounted as firm part thereof to be distributed and Dispos'd of in the same manner. ITEM I do Give and Bequeath unto my slave Wench named Minga the sum of Twenty Pagodas and her Liberty and to her son Antonio the sum of Forty Pagodas and to all her children Males and Females their Liberty. ITEM I do Give and Bequeath to my slave Wench named Francisca the sum of Twenty pagodas and her Liberty; also to all her Children their Liberty, Item I do Give, and Bequeath to my son Edward Fowke my slave Boy Named Placebo and to all the rest of my slaves whether male or Females; I do hereby Give them their Freedom and Liberty, No person whatsoever haveing any Claim or Title to any of them, nor shall hereafter have by Virtue of this my Last Will and Testament, I also Give and Bequeath to my former slave Wench named MAGDELANA in regard that she hath serv'd my Wife and self many years the sum of Twenty Pagodas. ITEM I do give and Bequeath to Peter Blacknall Watchmaker in London the sum of Thirty pounds sterl⁵. AND WHEREAS I have Given all my Children the sum of One Thousand pagodas each for the small presents made to them by their God fathers or God Mothers at their Baptism to make them equal in ther [*sic*] Fortunes But to my Daughter Sophia Holland, I Gave her Five Hundred Pagodas more at her marriage, also Five hundred more to each of my sons Edward Joseph and Francis : so That I have hitherto made an equal Distribution of what part of my Estate I can spare them in my Life time. I do therefore Will Order and Direct that after my Funeral Charges, and Lawfull Debts are Discharg'd; also the Legacys and Bequests herein mention'd, I WILL I Order and do Direct that the Residue or remaining part of my Estate both real and personal be equally Divided among my Four Children, namely my sons Edward. Joseph, and Francis Fowke whom I have appointed Executors to this my Last Will and Testament as afores^d. together and my aforenam'd Daughter Sophia and her Lawfull Issue, I do further Will Order and hereby Direct that all my Houses, House furniture silver and Gold plate Jewels Goods and all things that it hath pleas'd God to Bless one with at my Departure from this Life be fairly sold at auction or publick outcry and the nett Fourth part thereof I do hereby Leave and Bequeath to each of my Four Well beloved Children aforenamed. Upon the sale of my houses, I would enjoin them as well as advise them to prevent any future Disputes, or Quarrels, or Law suits to be very carefull and Exact in the measuring of the Grounds and Walls to be mention'd in the Bills of Sale to whom they must belong; which, in my Opinion the most Friendly, and Neighbourly way would be to make them all party-Walls, that is to say, and my meaning is. The Walls that part 'em to belong to One house as well as to that adjoining; This I only mention by way of advice But this particular I leave to their own discretion Only I would further advise êm to mention this in the Titles or Bills of Sale that neither party shall have the priviledge or power to strike out any sort of Lights, or break down such party Walls without the mutual consent given by Each other in Writeing, which is the thing I would do myself was. I to Dispose of, or sell them in my Life time I do further Will and Direct that whatsoever person or persons of my Legatees herein named shall Dye before his, her's or their Legacys are made payable by Virtue of this my Last Will and Testament it shall be Lawfull for my said Executors to bring the same to the Credit of my Estate and be accounted part thereof : The same I do say and Direct by and of the shares belonging to my Four Children herein aforenamed; that is to say whatsoever person or persons of them shall depart this Life before the Distri-bution of their shares as aforesaid that share or shares shall by Virtue hereof devolve to the surviveing or remaining person or persons of them in Equal shares, and to his, her's, or their Lawfully Issue—So haveing thus Disposed of all my Temporal Blessings I recomend my Dear Children to the Favour and Blessing of God whom I Beseech in his due time to send us all a Blessed Departure; and afterward, a joyfull Resurrection both of Soul and Body unto Life Eternal ALL the foregoing being Wrote with my own hand, and upon these Three sides of Paper, which I do

Do hereby ratifie, allow and confirm to be my last will and testament and annuling all other Will or Wills that might have been by me formerly made and this only to be regarded and fulfill'd to which I have set my hand side on the Fourth side of this sheet of paper in Fort St George in this City ofMarasspatnam this fourrth day of July One Thousand and Sevne Hundred and Forty Five.

SIGNED & SEALED PUBLISHED AND DECLARED buy the Testator to be his last will and testament in the presence of us and by us signed in the presence of the Testator and of each other there being no stamped paper procurable.

*Randall Fowke (LS)*

# Appendix IV
## Relationships of the Hollands & Fowkes

John Holland (1658–1721), merchant and banker, was born in London, the elder son of Captain Philip Holland, a professional sailor. The family was originally from Colchester, Essex.

In 1687 he married Jane Fowke (c.1669–1740), the only daughter of the second marriage of Walter Fowke MD, of Brewood Hall and Little Wyrley, Staffordshire. Brewood Hall became John and Jane's principal home, where they raised their three children: Richard (b. 1688), Jane (b. 1690), and Fowke (b. 1700). It would be convenient if either Richard or Fowke were the father of John and Esther Holland who married Edward and Sophia Fowke, the children of Randal, out in Madras; unfortunately, in the case of Richard, see below, this does not appear to be the case. Nevertheless, the connections between the two names over several generations give cause for curiosity. It is not beyond the realms of possibility that Edward Fowke, apothecary, the father of Randal who was murdered in Cork, was the older brother, cousin or uncle of Jane Fowke who married John Holland.

In 1695, together with various London Scots, John secured political backing for an act in the Scottish Parliament to set up a bank in Scotland under the name of the 'the Bank of Scotland'. It was founded with limited liability for shareholders and a nominal capital of £100,000 sterling of which the initial trading capital was £10,000. It was also given a monopoly over banking in Scotland for a period of twenty-one years. John was its first governor when it opened for business in February 1696.

John died at Brewood Hall on 30 November 1721 and was interred in the Fowke family vault at Brewood. His will was proved on 4 May 1722. Jane, his wife, died on 24 December 1740, having been predeceased by all her children.

His son Richard Holland (1688–1730), medical writer, was born in London and educated at St Catharine's College, Cambridge, where he graduated BA in 1709, MA in 1712, and MD in 1723. He and his father drew up a scheme for the establishment of a bank in Ireland similar to that in Scotland, but the scheme was not taken up. Holland inherited an estate in Ashdown Forest, Sussex. He was admitted as a candidate of the College of Physicians on 25 June 1724, a fellow on 25 June 1725, and was censor in 1728. He was elected a fellow of the Royal Society on 30 November 1726. He wrote Observations on the Small Pox, or, An Essay to Discover a More Effectual Method of Cure (1728), to which John Chandler wrote an anonymous reply in 1729. Richard Holland died, unmarried, at Shrewsbury, Shropshire, on 29 October 1730.

# Bibliography

**ARCHIVES**
**British Library, India Office Select Materials**
Eur D456: Correspondence of the Fowke, Benn, Walsh and
Maskelyne familes.

EUR, Kaye: Minor Collections, Fowke Mss: Handlists, an abstract
of the Fowke Mss.

HEIC, Court Records, Folio 5, Law Case No 31.

Mss Eur 032, *Memoir of Margaret Elizabeth Benn-Walsh (née Fowke)*, by
her son, John Benn-Walsh .

**Private collection belonging to Francis Fowke** (brother of the
author).
*Letters, Margaret Benn Walsh to Francis Fowke, 1790-1803.*


**BOOKS, WEBSITE AND JOURNALS**

Anonymous (1786): *The Trial of Joseph Fowke, Francis Fowke, Maha
Rajah Nundocomar, and Roy Rada Churn, for a Conspiracy against
Warren Hastings Esq. and that of Joseph Fowke, Maha Rajah
Nundocomar, and Roy Rada Churn, for a Conspiracy against Richard
Barwell Esq. to* ... Harvard Law School Library, Monograph,
HAR02564.

Bence-Jones, Mark (1974): *Clive of India*: London, Constable & Co.

Beveridge, Henry (2018): *The Trial of Maharaja Nanda Kumar*:
Forgotten Books.

Boswell, James (1831): *The Life of Samuel Johnson*, London, John
Murray.

Busteed, H. E. (1908): *Echoes from Old Calcutta*: New Delhi, Rupa & Co.

Chambers, Robert (1998): *Law, Literature and Empire*: Wisconsin, The University of Wisconsin Press.

Church of South India, the Family of (2015): *CSI St. Mary's Church*: Chennai, The Synod Secretariat.

Dalrymple, William (2019): *The Anarchy*: London, Bloomsbury.

Dampier, William (1999): *A New Voyage Round the World*: London, Humming Bird Press.

*Dictionary of National Biography*, entries for Joseph Fowke, John Walsh, Robert Clive, Edmund Masquelyne and others: Oxford University Press.

Dodwell, Henry (1920): *Dupleix and Clive, the Beginning of Empire*: London, Methuen & Co.

Dodwell, Henry (1926): *The Nabobs of Madras*: London, Williams and Norgate Ltd.

Dyson, Ketaki Kushari (1978): *A Various Universe, a Study of the Journals and Memoirs of British Men and Women in the Indian Subcontinent, 1765-1856*: New Delhi, Oxford University Press.

Edwards, P J: *Great Uncle Colonel Walsh* MP: University of Canberra.

Eileen and Harry Green (1973): *The Fowkes of Boughrood Castle*: Tenby.

Fay, Eliza, ed. E. M. Forster (1986): *Original Letters from India*: London, The Hogarth Press.

Feiling, Keith (1966): *Warren Hastings*: London, Macmillan.

Forde, Colonel Lionel (1910): *Lord Clive's Right Hand Man, A Memoir of Colonel Francis Forde*: London, Forgotten Books.

Ford, David Nash: *Royal Berkshire History:*
http://www.berkshirehistory.com/castles/warfield_park.html

*Gentleman's Magazine* Vol. 82 part 1 & Vol. 87.

Gopal, Ram (1963): *How the British Occupied Bengal*: Bombay, Asia Publishing House.

Gores, Steven J. (2000): *Psychosocial Spaces, Verbal and Visual Readings of British Culture 1750-1820*: Detrot, Wayne State University Press.

Harvey, Robert (1998): *Clive*: London, Hodder and Stoughton.

Hickman, Katie (2019): *She-Merchants, Buccaneers & Gentlewomen, British Women in India*: London, Virago Press.

Higgit, Rebekah (ed) (2014): *Maskelyne, Astronomer Royal*: London, National Maritime Museum.

Ives, Edward (1773): *A Voyage from England to India in the Year 1754*: London, Edward

and Charles Dilly.

*Journal of the Royal Society of Antiquaries of Ireland:* Notes and Queries, Vol 2.

Keay, John (1991): *The Honourable Company*: London, Harper Collins.

Keay, John (1991): *The Honourable Company*: London, Harper Collins.

Love, Henry Davison (1913): *Vestiges of Old Madras*, Vols 1 & 2: Chennai, J. Murray.

Malcolm, John (1836): *Life of Robert, Lord Clive*: London, John Murray.

Martineau, Alfred (1920): *Dupleix et l'Inde Française, 1722–1741:* Paris, Édouard Champion.

Muthiah, S. (2014): *Madras Rediscovered*: Chennai, EastWest.

Parkes, Fanny, ed. William Dalrymple (2002): *Begums, Thugs & White Mughals, the Journals of Fanny Parkes*: London, Sickle Moon Books.

Parthasarathi, Prasannan (2001): *The Transition to a Colonial Economy*: Cambridge University Press, Studies in Indian History & Society.

Piccolino, Marco (2003): *The Taming of the Ray*: Leo S. Olschki, Florence.

Quennell, Peter (ed) (1975): *Memoirs of William Hickey*: London, Routledge & Kegan Paul Ltd.

Robins, Nick (2012): *The Corporation that Changed the World*: London, Pluto Press.

Spear, Percival (1963) : *The Nabobs*: London, Oxford University Press.

Stephen, Sir James Fitzjames (1885): *The Story of Nuncomar and the Impeachment of Sir Elijah Impey*: London, Macmillan & Co.

Strachey, John (2010): *Hastings and the Rohilla War*: London, Kessinger Publishing.

Tharoor, Shashi (2017): *Inglorious Empire:* London, Penguin Books.

Trimingham, John Spencer (1964): *Islam in East Africa*: Oxford, Clarendon Press.

Various young Londoners (2010): *Plassey's Legacy*: London, The Brick Lane Circle.

Vickery, Amanda (1998): *The Gentleman's Daughter*: Yale University Press.

Walsh, John (1773): *Of The Electric Property of the Torpedo*: The Philosophical Transactions, Royal Society of London.

Watts, William (1760): *Memoirs of the Revolution in Bengal*: London, printed for A. Millar.

Woodfield, Ian (2000): *Music of the Raj*: Oxford, Oxford University Press.

# Index

BV - #0010 - 090421 - C0 - 203/133/11 - PB - 9781913425449 - Gloss Lamination